From
DIFFICULT
TEACHERS...
to
DYNAMIC
TEAMS

We dedicate this book to our mothers and grandmothers whose sacrifices and courage paved the way for us. We thank the many women and men who have mentored and nurtured us along the way with a special thanks to our longtime and dear friends, Shirley and Peggy, who continue to love, encourage, and support us even in those rare instances when we are "difficult."

From
DIFFICULT TEACHERS...
to
DYNAMIC TEAMS

Barbara L. Brock
Marilyn L. Grady

A JOINT PUBLICATION

For information:

Corwin
A SAGE Company
2455 Teller Road
Thousand Oaks, California 91320
(800) 233-9936
Fax: (800) 417-2466
www.corwinpress.com

SAGE India Pvt. Ltd.
1 Oliver's Yard
55 City Road
London EC1Y 1SP
United Kingdom

SAGE Ltd.
B 1/I 1 Mohan Cooperative
    Industrial Area
Mathura Road,
    New Delhi 110 044
India

SAGE Asia-Pacific Pte. Ltd.
33 Pekin Street #02-01
Far East Square
Singapore 048763

Printed in the United States of America.

Library of Congress Cataloging-in-Publication Data

Brock, Barbara L.
From difficult teachers . . . to dynamic teams/Barbara L. Brock, Marilyn L. Grady.
    p. cm.
"A Joint Publication With National Association of Elementary School Principals."
Includes bibliographical references and index.
ISBN 978-1-4129-1346-1 (cloth: alk. paper)
ISBN 978-1-4129-1347-8 (pbk. : alk. paper)
    1. Teacher effectiveness—United States. 2. Teachers—In-service training—United States. 3. Teachers—United States—Discipline. 4. Teacher-principal relationships—United States. 5. Communication in education—United States. I. Grady, Marilyn L. II. National Association of Elementary School Principals (U.S.) III. Title.

LB2832.2.B762009
371.1—dc22

2009004909

This book is printed on acid-free paper.

09   10   11   12   13   10 9 8 7 6 5 4 3 2 1

Acquisitions Editor:	Debra Stollenwerk
Associate Editor:	Julie McNall
Production Editor:	Libby Larson
Copy Editor:	Jeannette McCoy
Typesetter:	C&M Digitals (P) Ltd.
Proofreader:	Charlotte J. Waisner
Indexer:	Jean Casalegno
Cover Designer:	Lisa Riley
Graphic Designer:	Rose Storey

Contents

List of Resources   vii

Acknowledgments   ix

About the Authors   xi

Introduction   1

Part I: Identification and Understanding   5

1. **Understanding Difficult Teachers**   7
   Who Are They?   7
   How Did They Get This Way?   13
   What Do They Want?   15
   What Effect Do They Have?   17

2. **Difficult Teachers, Difficult Behaviors**   25
   Chronic Complainers   25
   Negative Teachers   31
   Inflexible Teachers   32
   Noncompliant Teachers   34
   Gossipers   35
   Anarchists   40
   Snipers   42
   Bullies   43
   Noisemakers   46
   Selfish Teachers   48

Part II: Solutions and Strategies   49

3. **Facilitating Behavior Change: Conversations, Warnings, and Improvement Plans**   51
   Before a Problem Occurs   51
   How to Encourage Behavior Change   56
   When Conversations Fail   64

4. Am I Contributing to the Problem?   **71**

Why Are Some Principals "Difficult"?   73

Could Your Behavior Be Considered Difficult?   76

Fertile Ground for Difficult Teachers   78

Gender-Related Differences in Difficult Behavior   82

Strategies for Change   86

Part III: Prevention   **91**

5. Interpersonal Skills That Help   **93**

Listening to Understand   95

Speaking for Understanding   99

Body Language   102

Diffusing Emotionally Charged Conversations   103

6. Creating a Culture of Teamwork   **111**

Building a Positive Culture   112

Focusing on Positive Teachers   115

Creating a Spirit of Teamwork   122

Rewarding Positive People   124

Parting Thoughts: From Difficult Teachers
to Dynamic Teamwork   141

Resources   **143**

References   **153**

Index   **157**

List of Resources

CHAPTER 3

Behavior Change Plan   58, 144

Behavior Change Plan for Teacher A   59

Strategies for Dealing With Difficult Teachers   60

CHAPTER 4

Causes of Difficult Behavior in Principals   73

Part 1: Teacher's Evaluation of the
Principal's Performance   89, 145

Part 2: Teacher's Evaluation of the
Principal's Performance   90, 146

CHAPTER 5

Nonverbal Cues   103

Teacher's Evaluation of the Principal: Listening Skills   108, 147

Teacher's Evaluation of the Principal: Speaking Skills   109, 148

CHAPTER 6

Appreciation Assessment   127, 149

Identification of Teacher Leaders   132, 150

Your Communication Strategies   135, 151

Teacher Assistance   140, 152

Acknowledgments

During the writing of this book, we have enjoyed the support of our families to whom we express our sincere gratitude: Michael, David, Eric, and J. D. Brock, and Justin and Elizabeth Grady. We have also enjoyed the support of a team of people whom we would like to acknowledge and thank for their assistance in preparing this book: the principals and teachers who shared their time and experiences with us: Suzanne Becking, Instructional Designer at the University of Nebraska-Lincoln for her assistance in the preparation of the manuscript; Minisa Chapman-Huls, doctoral student at the University of Nebraska-Lincoln for her valuable research assistance; former Creighton University student, Anna Mattia, for her valuable research assistance; Creighton University librarians, Lynn Schneiderman, for the many successful "treasure hunts," and Mary Nash and Geri Chase for their consistent helpfulness; Debra Stollenwerk, our editor at Corwin, for guiding the process; and to the following peer reviewers for sharing their valuable insights with us:

Patricia Bowman
Retired Principal/LAUSD
Adjunct Professor UCLA
Los Angeles, CA

Roxanne Cardona
Principal
Public School System, CSA, ASCD
New York, NY

Dr. Nora G. Friedman
Principal
South Grove Elementary School
Syosset, NY

Patrick M. Jenlink
Professor of Doctoral Studies and Director,
    Education Research Center
Stephen F. Austin State University
Nacogdoches, TX

Kim E. Vogel
Principal
Parkdale Elementary School
Parkdale, OR

About the Authors

 **Barbara L. Brock** is Professor of Education and former Chair of the Education Department and Director of School Administration at Creighton University. Her research interests include the career development of teachers and principals. She is coauthor, with Marilyn L. Grady, of *From First-Year to First-Rate: Principals Guiding Beginning Teachers; Developing a Teacher Induction Plan; Launching Your First Principalship; Avoiding Burnout: A Principal's Guide to Keeping the Fire Alive; Rekindling the Flame: Principals Combating Teacher Burnout;* and *Principals in Transition: Tips for Surviving Succession.* Her work has been published in a number of book chapters and journals, including the *Journal of School Leadership, Clearing House,* the *Journal of the Midwestern Educational Research Association, Educational Considerations,* and *Catholic Education: A Journal of Inquiry and Practice.* She presents nationally and internationally on topics related to the career development of educators.

Dr. Brock's educational experience includes teaching and administration at the K–12 and college levels. She received a bachelor of arts degree in art education from Briar Cliff College, Sioux City, Iowa; a master of science degree in education from Creighton University; and a doctor of education degree in administration, curriculum, and instruction from the University of Nebraska-Lincoln. She is a member of the American Educational Research Association, the National Council of Professors of Educational Administration, Phi Delta Kappa, and Alpha Sigma Nu, the Jesuit National Honor Society. Her e-mail address is bbrock@creighton.edu.

 **Marilyn L. Grady**, PhD, is Professor of Educational Administration at the University of Nebraska-Lincoln (UNL). She is the author or coauthor of 23 books, including *Getting It Right From the Start: The Principal's Guide to Early Childhood Education* (2009), *194 High-Impact Letters for Busy Principals* (2006) and *20 Biggest Mistakes Principals Make and How to Avoid Them* (2004). Her research areas include leadership, the principalship, and superintendent-board relations. She has more than 175 publications to her credit. She is the editor of the *Journal of Women in Educational Leadership* and *Contemporary Issues in Education*. Her editorial board service has included *Educational Administration Quarterly, Rural Educator, Journal of At-Risk Issues, Journal of School Leadership, Advancing Women in Leadership Online Journal, Journal for Rural School and Community Renewal, International Journal of Learning*, and *Journal for a Just and Caring Education*. She is the recipient of the Stanley Brzezinski Research Award, the National Council of Professors of Educational Administration's Living Legend Award, and UNL's award for Outstanding Contributions to the Status of Women.

Dr. Grady coordinates an annual conference on women in educational leadership that attracts international attendance and is in its 22nd year. She has served on the executive board of the National Council of Professors of Educational Administration, the Center for the Study of Small/Rural Schools, and Phi Delta Kappa Chapter 15. She is a member of the American Educational Research Association, the International Academy of Educational Leaders, the National Rural Education Association, the National Council of Professors of Educational Administration, Phi Delta Kappa, and the Horace Mann League.

Dr. Grady has been an administrator in K–12 schools as well as at the college and university levels. She received her bachelor's degree in history from Saint Mary's College, Notre Dame, Indiana, and her doctorate in educational administration with a specialty in leadership from The Ohio State University. Her e-mail address is mgrady1@unl.edu.

Introduction

We believe that teachers are a school's greatest resource: the most important factor in student achievement and ultimately school success. We began our careers as teachers, spent a number of years in PreK–12 administrative positions, and continue our teaching roles today as university professors. We are advocates of best teaching and administrative practices. That is the reason why in this book, we write about a sensitive topic: difficult teachers.

We know from the literature, our own research, and our teaching and administrative experiences, that we write about a very small number of the teachers in schools. In most schools, there is a core of dedicated, enthusiastic, and generous teachers who volunteer for or are assigned more than their share of work. Most school leaders dream of having a faculty composed of enthusiastic, positive, and cooperative teachers. The dream, however, is rarely a reality. Although most teachers are hardworking, enthusiastic, and cooperative, faculties often include at least one or two teachers whose behavior is characterized as "difficult." This small but often powerful group irritates colleagues, disheartens students, and provokes endless headaches for even the most seasoned of school leaders. Left unchecked, the behavior of difficult teachers seeps into every aspect of the school, disrupting the teamwork required in effective learning communities and ultimately threatening student achievement.

Although you cannot change teachers' personalities or behavior habits, you can learn to influence teachers to change their own behaviors. Thus, our approach to the topic is a positive, generative one. We believe that school leaders can assist teachers in addressing difficult behaviors. Our emphasis is on what can be accomplished rather than on the barriers that prevent action. The ideal is to communicate with them in such a way that they change themselves. By learning how to work with teachers when they are behaving inappropriately, you can defuse their power. The proactive approach minimizes or prevents the development and occurrence of unacceptable behaviors through positive team-building strategies.

(Note: For the sake of convenience and in order to depict what the behavior looks like, we sometimes use the term "difficult teachers." In order to understand the behaviors and determine solutions for them, however, it is important to separate the behavior from the person. In reality, people are not difficult; rather, they behave in difficult ways.)

The contents of the book are based on our experiences as school leaders, a review of the literature, conversations with teachers, and interviews with school principals. We interviewed and collected data from 50 elementary and secondary principals in public and nonpublic schools who identified the most troublesome behaviors in their organizations, shared their solutions for redirecting these behaviors, and suggested strategies for team-building. The quotations in the book are from the conversations with teachers and the interviews with principals.

PURPOSE AND
ORGANIZATION OF THIS BOOK

This book will help you identify and adopt effective communication strategies for dealing with difficult, disruptive, and negative teachers. Your perseverance in changing resistant behaviors will yield a repertoire of communication strategies that will serve you in a variety of situations. In the process, you may discover personal behaviors that you wish to modify. Additionally, the book will help you identify team-building strategies that will minimize the emergence of negative and other troublesome behaviors.

Part I of the book includes the identification of problematic behaviors and examines the reasons that teachers behave inappropriately. Part II includes solutions and strategies used by experienced principals to redirect inappropriate behavior and reduce the negative power it generates. Part III offers suggestions to prevent the development of negative teachers and toxic subcultures by building a culture of shared leadership, collegiality, and team spirit; all of which are essential for successful teamwork.

SPECIAL FEATURES

Special features of the book include the following:

- Quotes from the teachers and principals we interviewed.
- A *Take Action* section, at the end of each chapter, guides principals to immediate "next" steps. These suggestions provide ways for school leaders to implement the material presented in the chapter. The action focus encourages reader involvement with the content of the text.
- The charts and assessment forms, found in Chapters 3, 4, 5, and 6, and in the Resources section in the back of the book, are key tools for busy school leaders. These resources move the content from prose to practice.

A FINAL NOTE ABOUT THE AUDIENCE FOR THIS BOOK

Throughout the book we use the word *principal* as an example of a school leader. However, the book is written for all practitioners in educational leadership positions: teacher leaders, aspiring school leaders, and professors of educational administration. If your staff is always cheerful, positive, and cooperative, consider yourself blessed and read no further. If, however, your staff includes teachers whose behavior provokes headaches, anguish, and sleepless nights, read on. . . . This book is written for you.

Part I

Identification and Understanding

CHAPTER ONE

Understanding Difficult Teachers

The ability to work with people is as purchasable a commodity as coffee or sugar, but I'd pay more for it than any other ability under the sun.

—John D. Rockefeller

○ Who are they?

○ How did they get this way?

○ What do they want?

○ What effect do they have?

WHO ARE THEY?

- *The Complainer:* I have all these problems. . . .
- *The Negative:* Been there, done that; nothing works.
- *The Inflexible:* It's worked for years, and I'm not changing!
- *The Noncompliant:* Oh, did you need that this week?
- *The Gossiper:* Have you heard . . . ?
- *The Anarchist:* I can run this school better than . . .

(Continued)

(Continued)

- *The Noisemakers:* I'm calling the media, the school board, the PTA.
- *The Sniper:* Gotcha!
- *The Backbiter:* I will be your friend . . . until later. . . .
- *The Teacher Tyrant:* This is my classroom; it's my way!
- *The Intimidator:* I am right . . . your idea is stupid!
- *The Selfish:* It isn't my turn . . . .

Most teachers are cooperative, positive, and hardworking. Only 5% to 10% of teachers display negative attitudes and disruptive behaviors (Brock & Grady, 2006). Although small in number, difficult teachers create messy problems and big headaches that demand a disproportionate amount of time and attention from school leaders. Their behaviors can damage faculty morale, threaten school culture, and thwart attainment of institutional goals. Most important, their behaviors can interfere with student learning. When displayed in the classrooms, their behaviors are harmful to students and provoke angry responses from parents. Educators sometimes avoid mentioning problems in the profession, fearing that doing so casts aspersion on all teachers. Just the opposite is true. Identifying problem behavior and seeking corrective solutions promotes desirable benefits for everyone.

Although it is not something we like to admit, at times most of us are "difficult." The *Oxford Dictionary* (1997) defines the word "difficult," as it relates to a person, as "not easy to please; uncooperative; or troublesome" (p. 207). We all have days when that definition might apply to us—when we are grumpy, when we sulk because we don't get "our way," when we complain about a change at work, when we criticize our employer, or when we are less than supportive of a new initiative. And even the best of us have, on occasion, relished a bit of juicy gossip or reacted venomously to a colleague's success.

But there is an important difference between teachers who are occasionally difficult and those who are persistently difficult (Glickman, Gordon, & Ross-Gordon, 2009). A difficult teacher's problem behavior is habitual, affects many people, and is routinely perceived as troublesome by a wide variety of individuals

(Bramson, 1981). One author explained, [You can determine if a person is truly difficult by asking yourself] ". . . would the problem go away if so-and-so went for a hike in the harbor wearing cement overshoes . . . ?" (Negotiation Skills Company, 2003). Principals in our study were much kinder in their terminology but nonetheless described troubling behaviors. One principal described difficult teachers as:

> Teachers who use poor judgment in discipline/supervision issues, are negative, verbally abusive to students, have signs of mental illness, have difficulty differentiating to meet the needs of individuals, want kids with discipline problems out, turn small problems with colleagues into big problems, frequently share negative comments about students/job with others.

Other principals agreed, explaining,

> I think another cause of difficult behavior is just self-absorption in general. People forget they are the adults. They are here for the students, not the other way around. There is a feeling of "what have you done for me lately?" That bothers me.

Another principal suggested that for some teachers, "difficult" behaviors were seasonal. She called it "March/February Madness," explaining "most teachers become more difficult during this time."

Sometimes difficult teachers are not consciously aware that their behaviors are inappropriate or how they affect others. However, on occasion, it can be deliberate. One principal reported a situation in which a small group of teachers deliberately ostracized and bullied another teacher whom they wanted to leave the school. When the principal removed the "ringleader" of the bullies from the school, the problem stopped.

Another principal reported a teacher on her staff whose mission in life was to thwart her leadership. She engaged in malicious gossiping, criticized the principal behind her back, and lobbied teachers to follow her lead. When the principal pointed out that she was running the school and suggested that the teacher become a principal herself if she wanted to be in charge, the teacher left the school.

Although the nuances of human behavior are complex and impossible to simplistically categorize, some general patterns of difficult teachers exist. Principals identified the following behavior patterns as problematic.

- **Complaining:** Complainers persistently voice negative comments about students, their job, the principal, and the school. They moan about their personal lives, children, and spouses. Nobody has it as "bad" as they do. Although they gripe and moan incessantly, they do nothing to improve the situation. They relish sympathy and usually hang out with other complainers with whom they enjoy daily pity parties. Their favorite haunt is the faculty lounge.
- **Negativity:** These individuals throw a "wet blanket" on any new proposal. Their typical response to a new idea is, "That will never work" or "We tried that once before and it didn't work." One principal described negative teachers as ". . . my least favorite because they sap the strength right out of me" (Brock & Grady, 2006). Just a few negative teachers, especially if they have strong personalities, can quickly lower faculty morale. Additionally, their tendency to seek out new teachers to tell them "what it's really like" makes negative teachers destructive to the professional growth and development of new teachers. They join the complainers in the faculty lounge to create a toxic environment.
- **Inflexibility:** Inflexible teachers are unwilling to change or resistant to growth opportunities. Inflexible teachers are stuck in a rut of mediocrity. Their attitude is, "I've done it this way for years, and it works for me. I'm not changing, and you can't make me." When inflexible teachers band together, they form an effective bottleneck or roadblock to new initiatives.
- **Noncompliance:** There are two types of teachers who do not comply: those who are openly, belligerently noncompliant and those who are quietly and passively noncompliant. In either case, they do not follow the rules and do not fulfill their obligations. The belligerent are noisier about their noncompliance. They openly announce their displeasure to you and to anyone who will listen. The passive noncompliant teachers say nothing, but engage in practices such as

chronically missing deadlines, "forgetting" to complete required forms, or arriving late for meetings.

- **Gossiping:** Most schools have at least one "Chatty Cathy and Chatty Charlie." These teachers love to be the first to know and share. They revel in the attention garnered through their newfound information. Unfortunately, factual accuracy is not terribly important to them. There are two kinds of gossipers: those who gossip because they enjoy the attention and those who gossip because they have a malicious intent. Both kinds of gossiping can cause damage; however, the attention seekers are usually oblivious to the trail of damage. Some nonmalicious gossipers even attempt to share their juicy tidbits with their principals. One principal admitted, "I cringe when [a gossiper] comes in my direction" (Brock & Grady, 2006). Malicious gossipers are another story. They deliberately construct and spread untruths for the purpose of inflicting damage to another's reputation. Often their target is the principal or some other member of the administrative team, and their goal is to damage the leader's credibility. Although both varieties of gossipers create headaches for principals, the malicious gossiper can inflict serious damage to an administrator's career.

- **Anarchy:** These teachers either disagree with and/or do not like the principal. They freely share their sentiments with anyone who will listen to them. Their goal is to undermine the principal with criticism, discourage cooperation, and in some cases, incite anarchy. Malicious gossip, backbiting, and sniping are their tools. A few well-planted untruths combined with malicious comments during faculty meetings can effectively diminish trust in a principal. Teachers bent on anarchy destroy faculty cohesiveness and undermine a principal's leadership, especially if they gain followers. Inexperienced teachers and teachers prone to negative behavior are particularly vulnerable to their influence and become prime targets and willing followers.

- **Noisemaking:** Noisemakers, when thwarted, may seek to call attention to their plight by contacting the media, school board, or PTA. They want attention, validation of their plight, and possibly revenge for the real or imagined "wrongs" they have suffered. They can undermine the credibility of a new or inexperienced principal with the school's publics. Internally, they can instigate toxic subcultures that undermine the principal's authority and threaten school goals.

- **Sniping:** Snipers take potshots at the principal during meetings by making rude statements or critical comments. Their behavior is designed to arouse an emotional response (e.g., confusion, anger) and thereby fluster the speaker. Any sign of weakness on the part of the principal fuels their behavior and incites fellow snipers, who generally sit together to enjoy the festivities. A sniper with a band of malcontents can disrupt a meeting and make a principal appear ineffective.
- **Backbiting/Backstabbing:** These individuals are sweet to your face but deadly when your back is turned. The backstabber deceives the leader with friendliness in order to gain trust and information. The information is then twisted and used to sabotage, discredit, embarrass, or somehow diminish the leader's credibility.
- **Tyrannical:** These teachers instigate countless calls to the principal from angry parents and upset students. They consider their classrooms as little empires or fiefdoms over which they alone preside. In their eyes, they are always right; parents and students are always wrong. Middle ground or gray areas do not exist in their black and white world. Consequently, they are the source of poor relationships and constant conflicts with parents and students. Left unchecked, their behavior damages students, relationships with parents, and the school's reputation in the community.
- **Intimidating:** Intimidators think they know it all and display their superiority through condescension toward colleagues. They are always right and have little regard for the opinions and feelings of others. They routinely intimidate others through their verbal and nonverbal behaviors. Some intimidators make condescending or cutting comments that stifle discussion; others are skilled at doing so nonverbally with raised eyebrows, smirks, and looks of boredom or disbelief. Their goal is to make others feel stupid and thus silence them. Their power increases when surrounded by

an audience of like-minded friends. One administrator acknowledged,

> In 21 years as an elementary principal, my most challenging staff problem was a teacher who could not get along with other adults. Her style was intimidating to others. She was always right. Her adult social skills and personality were impossible to correct. (Brock & Grady, 2006)

- **Selfish/Self-Centered:** These individuals view their jobs very narrowly. If a task is not expressly identified in their contract, it is not their problem or their responsibility. These teachers are frugal with their time and are not interested in participating in, much less volunteering for, school projects and initiatives. The often-heard refrains from self-centered teachers are, "Why do I have to do it?" "It isn't my turn." "Not my job." Their approach to teaching is that of an hourly employee rather than as a professional educator. They do not exude interest in improving the school or the profession. One principal explained, "[difficult teachers] want 'ease for self' more than learning for students."

HOW DID THEY GET THIS WAY?

How do difficult teachers get that way? Although hard to believe, most difficult teachers were not born that way. Each of us is genetically predisposed to certain behavioral tendencies and characteristics. Most of our behavior is learned through interactions with others (Aldrich, 2002). Predisposition plays a role in that some individuals are more inclined to be irritable, impatient, inflexible, and pessimistic, while others are calm, patient, adaptable, and optimistic. Predisposition or temperament, however, does not dictate behavior once one reaches adulthood. Adults may be influenced by temperament, but they choose their behaviors.

Difficult teachers want to control their environment. As children, they learned through trial and error which behaviors were rewarded and which ones were punished. A behavior that led to the desired result was reinforced and thus repeated. When children learn at an early age that difficult behaviors such as crying, tantrums, whining, complaining, and aggression are rewarded, these behaviors become part of their repertoire. Throughout childhood, adolescence, and into adulthood, early behaviors are refined, modified, and result in the behaviors adults exhibit when they are under stress or simply want to do things their way.

Some authors report that gender-related societal expectations and childhood games play a role in adult behavior, including inappropriate behavior. Boys and girls are treated differently from the moment they are born. They learn behavioral expectations from interactions with parents, teachers, other adults, and the media. Boys tend to play competitive, outdoor group games. Their games involve leaders, rules, winners, and losers. When participants disagree, decisions are made so the game can continue. Girls tend to play in pairs or small groups. Their games are usually cooperative and do not require leaders, rules, winners, and losers. When disagreements occur, the girls change the informal rules or play a different game. There are no winners or losers. Boys are exposed to and subsequently learn the important skills of assertive behavior and asking for what they need through childhood games. However, they also are more likely to be verbally or physically aggressive to a perceived enemy. Girls' play helps them acquire skills in communication and cooperation but does not aid them in their acquisition of assertive behavior and asking for what they need or want. Since physical and verbal aggression is socially unacceptable, girls may use passive-aggressive behaviors to sabotage their enemies by snubbing, exclusion, and malicious gossip (Heim, Murphy, & Golant, 2001).

Preservice teachers exhibit many of the behaviors they will display in their first teaching jobs. Professors often can identify aspiring teachers who will become a thorn in the side of a future administrator. Students who heave sighs of exasperation, roll their eyes, and glare at anyone who dares delay the end of class by asking a question are using intimidation skills that they may use at future faculty meetings. Noncompliant students whose assignments are chronically late but accompanied by colorful excuses are the noncompliant teachers of the future. Students who are negative, chronic complainers and gossipers will continue these behaviors as teachers. Without guidance, these teachers will be unaware of the inappropriateness of their behaviors and the potentially negative impact their behaviors may have on their careers. Preservice teacher training should include discussions of appropriate professional behavior with guidance offered to aspiring teachers who exhibit difficult behaviors.

WHAT DO THEY WANT?

A Rationale for Behavior

- Behaviors are chosen.
- Every behavior has a purpose.
- What worked in the past is repeated.

Difficult teachers want things their way. Some difficult teachers seek the enjoyment of creating havoc and thrive on the chaos they create, not caring whether the attention is positive or negative (Aldrich, 2002). They stir up a problem to gain attention and derive satisfaction from watching the havoc they reaped. They gain a psychological reward from attention, and they do not care if it is negative.

Whenever we communicate, we use one of four basic forms of behavior: assertive, aggressive, passive, or passive-aggressive. The behavior style we choose depends on what has worked for us in the past. According to Brinkman & Kirschner (2002), we select behaviors based on what we need to accomplish and the level of assertiveness the task requires. "For each of us there is a zone of normal or best behavior and exaggerated or worst behavior" (p. 15).

Although assertive behavior is the healthiest form, unfortunately, it is also the least used. Under stress, we often resort to unhealthier forms of behavior such as passive, aggressive, or passive-aggressive behaviors (Podesta & Sanderson, 1999). An examination of the four behavior types follows.

The healthiest behavior occurs when we are assertive or direct in expressing our needs and wants. Assertive individuals stand up for their rights but are sensitive to the rights of others. They express what they want or feel in a direct and honest manner. They ask questions, listen objectively, engage in dialogue, and examine available choices. Anger or hurt feelings do not dictate their behavior or their choices. The principal in the following conversation is using assertive communication skills.

Janice, the contract specifies that teachers are to be in their classroom by 8:00 a.m. each day. The last five days you have arrived at 8:15 a.m., leaving your students unsupervised. I need you to be there at 8:00 a.m. Is there some problem that is preventing you from fulfilling this requirement?

The passive style of behavior is characterized by inaction. Passive individuals are indecisive; they refuse to make choices and seldom express opinions. They avoid confrontation at all costs. Some passive people erroneously equate passivity with being a nice, unselfish person. Although passivity may be a positive choice, when the situation is not "worth the effort" or we do not care about the outcome, continual passivity at the expense of having our needs met is not healthy. Working with passive people is frustrating because we do not know what they want, and they judge others on how well they guess what their needs are (Podesta & Sanderson, 1999). Favorite responses of passive individuals include, "I don't care" and "you decide."

At the other extreme are individuals who use the aggressive style of behavior. They yell, complain, cry, accuse, blame, pout, or do whatever it takes to get their own way. They want control, and everyone else is expected to comply with their demands. Their weapons are hurt and anger. If you get in the way, you become the enemy to be conquered (Podesta & Sanderson, 1999).

For some individuals, passive-aggressive is the behavior style of choice. They are passive in avoiding direct confrontation but aggressive in acts of manipulation to get even. They act as if everything is fine to your face but engage in devious acts of sabotage behind the scenes (Podesta & Sanderson, 1999). Strategies included in their sabotage toward a school leader might include malicious gossip about the leader, withholding critical information, encouraging dissent among the faculty, sniping during faculty meetings—anything they can do to make the school leader appear ineffective.

None of us use one behavior choice exclusively. At one time or another, we probably use all forms of behavior. We do what has worked in the past. If in the past, the use of assertive behavior has worked for us, we probably rely on it for most situations. If, however, we have become accustomed to getting our way by using passive, aggressive, or passive-aggressive behavior to solve problems, then we will likely resort to one of these behaviors when under stress. The difficult teachers in schools want to do things when, if, and how they want to do them. They want to be in control of their work environment and in control of other people. They have adopted behavior styles that keep the people around them uncomfortable and disarmed (Bramson, 1981; Aldrich, 2002).

A Word of Caution

One should exercise caution before hastily labeling a teacher's behavior as difficult. Teachers are well-educated, intelligent individuals who have a different vantage point than that of the principal. They may be aware of problems that the principal has failed to notice. The difficult teacher may be the only person to recognize a problem that needs to be addressed or to be brave enough to announce, "The emperor has no clothes" (Andersen, 1837). Thus, it is prudent to investigate complaints and disagreements to determine if there is a kernel of truth before dismissing a teacher's behavior as difficult. Painful to admit, but sometimes the principal is considered difficult by the teachers or is inadvertently creating a situation that fosters difficult behavior.

WHAT EFFECT DO THEY HAVE?

Difficult teachers contribute to faculty and administrator stress and can eventually adversely affect physical health. They damage morale, destroy collegiality, thwart productivity, threaten school goals, and make administrators appear ineffective. In short, they are a major source of headaches for school leaders. In extreme cases, they contribute to teacher and sometimes principal attrition.

When the agenda of difficult teachers is to damage a principal's career, they can be ruthless in their quest. Male and female principals are suitable targets for teacher saboteurs. However, some researchers report that women leaders are more likely to be targets of indirect aggression by other women than are men. Acts of female sabotage usually take the form of passive-aggressive behavior such as malicious gossip, backbiting, and sniping; all of which are intended to undermine the female leader's authority and credibility. By contrast, difficult men are usually more overt and direct in their difficult behavior. Some authors' rationale for the differences in behavioral choices is the nature of women's relationships and societal expectations for females to be less outwardly aggressive than males (Chesler, 2001; Heim, Murphy, & Golant, 2001; Podesta & Sanderson, 1999). Since displays of outward aggressiveness are discouraged for female children, they adopt passive-aggressive behaviors when they want their way.

The women administrators in our studies surpassed the men in their reports of women teachers whose difficult behaviors included acts of sabotage against them. These women leaders responded with strong emotion toward the teachers and sometimes doubted their own decisions and actions. By contrast, most of the men and some of the women in our studies reported few incidents of sabotage, did not mention women teachers in particular, and did not report strong emotion related to the incidents. They did not report doubting their decisions and were more likely to place the teacher on an improvement plan.

The most destructive individuals are the difficult teachers who create a living hell in their classrooms. In their black and white world, there is no room for flexibility, understanding, or sensitivity to students. After all, they are always right; everyone else is wrong. They treat students as inferior beings and regard parents as inept and bothersome. Sarcasm, embarrassment, and harsh punishment are commonplace. Their behavior precipitates frequent conflicts with students and calls from angry parents. Some parents, however, avoid complaining or making waves because they fear retaliation on their children. Students who are "sentenced" to a year in the classrooms of these teachers learn little else than disdain for school and learning.

The behavior of difficult teachers keeps everybody on edge and off balance and thereby unable or reluctant to respond. Coworkers, administrators, and sometimes parents tend to ignore, avoid, appease, or tiptoe around difficult teachers to avoid unpleasantness or retaliation.

Although principals reported being quick to act when students were in jeopardy, some reported ignoring difficult behavior directed toward them or toward faculty members, hoping that it would simply go away. They did so for several reasons:

1. They wanted to avoid an unpleasant confrontation. Most of us do not enjoy confronting others about their failings,

especially if we suspect the person will not react favorably. Unfortunately, avoidance can be costly in terms of faculty morale, teacher burnout, goal attainment, and leadership credibility.

2. Many difficult teachers have a following or support system within the staff that may create additional unrest among the faculty, students, or parents. When difficult teachers are informal leaders among the faculty, they form negative subcultures of like-minded teachers. When you confront the leader, a posse of teachers from the negative subculture will rise to defend their leader. You will be vilified on all fronts but unable to justify your actions due to personnel confidentiality. One principal reported a situation in which the difficult teacher and her posse sent letters to parents and school board members citing unfair treatment and demanding termination of the principal. A few difficult teachers develop a following among parents or students. These teachers cultivate alliances with parents and students showing them only their best behavior. Parents and students have no idea that sweet Mrs. Smith becomes a tyrant who intimidates others during faculty meetings. When the teacher informs her followers of the confrontation, she becomes the sympathetic victim, and you become the evil principal—one who is bound to uphold the confidentiality of personnel information. One of the authors recalls being the recipient of letters from parents pleading the case of a "wonderful" teacher who was being terminated by a neighboring principal. Obviously, the parents had undertaken a mass mailing to save the teacher's job oblivious to any of the personnel issues that had factored into the decision.

3. Some school leaders are not certain what strategy will be effective. After all, little research on the topic has occurred, and there is no "bank of strategies" available for school leaders.

Ignoring the problem, however, is not an effective strategy. Ignoring the behaviors of difficult teachers magnifies stress, makes you feel and look powerless in the eyes of the faculty, and gives tacit approval to its continuance—condoning and sanction-ing it as acceptable. Instead of disappearing, difficult behavior will not only continue but will flourish, intensify, and become infec-tious if concerns are not brought into the open. Principals told us that difficult teachers, particularly those who are negative, "feed off each other" and that negative behaviors are contagious when "not directly dealt with by the administrator in a timely manner." They noted, "If the behavior is ignored, it may/will spread." By contrast, "if the leader steps in, writes someone up, or does a repri-mand, the behavior may stop."

Although some behaviors are annoying, they are harmless and can be ignored. However, avoidance as a solution for chroni-cally difficult teachers is not a good choice. Closely aligned with ignoring is appeasing a person by giving him what he wants. Although it is tempting to do this, especially with chronic whiners and complainers, this tactic also gives tacit approval to inappro-priate behavior and encourages it to flourish.

As one principal explained, "People continue to do what works for them until somebody says something." Failure to curtail the behavior establishes a fertile environment in which negative subcultures develop, thrive, and spread throughout the faculty. Gradually, negativity and disgruntlement become imbedded in the school culture.

Principals said,

> Teachers who are negative become toxic to others in the building [and] are very difficult to deal with. You know who they are . . . but it is very difficult to turn them around.

> I think toxic teachers can influence others just by wearing them down. They are just so negative and so relentless . . . that eventually they can create negativity in others. They want support for their negative feelings and thoughts and con-stantly seek others who might feel the same. (Brock & Grady, 2006, p. 10)

Principals noted, "Veteran teachers [with negative behaviors] have a tremendous impact on first, second, and third year [teachers]." They are the most vulnerable prey and most likely to become followers of negative leaders. One principal observed,

"Although most teachers don't agree with difficult behaviors, they may be hesitant to stand up to that type of person." Another principal explained, "Staff members who have difficult behaviors often try to intimidate other staff to be negative or be quiet. They tend to dominate conversations and meeting agendas. Eventually, some [staff] start believing what is being said . . . difficult behaviors can be contagious, especially if others perceive that 'the squeaky wheel gets the grease.'"

When negative and disruptive behaviors are left unchecked, entire faculties can become infected and form toxic subcultures (Peterson & Deal, 2002) that damage school culture, threaten goal attainment, and most importantly, interfere with student learning. One principal noted that difficult teachers often develop a "following or support system within the staff." Another principal explained, "One or two negative, subversive, or outspoken and aggressive teachers usually bring at least one [or more teachers] with them and affect all staff in terms of cohesiveness." One principal summarized the seriousness of the problem, "Teachers who are negative become toxic to others in the building [and] are very difficult to deal with. You know who they are . . . but it is very difficult to turn them around."

Negative and disruptive behavior may become contagious when

- Difficult behaviors are not promptly dealt with by the administrator.
- The faculty is not strong.
- Difficult teachers intimidate other staff to be negative or to be quiet.
- The difficult teacher is a leader among the faculty.
- Teachers are relatively new—in their first, second, and third years.
- Teachers are marginal in performance.

Teacher Attrition

The behavior of difficult teachers can contribute to teacher attrition, especially when the staff is largely young, inexperienced, and vulnerable. One administrator explained, "The [difficult] teacher kept latching on to young, inexperienced teachers and convincing them that it was a horrible school." Other administrators echoed similar problems: "I had an excellent first-year teacher leave teaching to go back to nursing school after one year with an especially difficult teammate" and "One teacher who couldn't stand . . . the confrontational, critical attitude of one staff member transferred out."

When student teachers are involved, the effects of a difficult teacher's behavior are particularly damaging. One principal explained,

> I had a very controlling teacher who wouldn't work with an assigned student teacher. Although I thought things were going well, they truly weren't. The student teacher went home in tears on a daily basis. The college contacted me and requested an alternative placement . . . we made that happen. (Brock & Grady, 2006)

The teachers we spoke with believed it is the responsibility of the principal to address the behavior of difficult teachers. They emphasized the importance of swift intervention to prevent damage to staff morale and collaborative efforts. Teachers were emphatic about the need for the principal to take direct action rather than wait for peers of the difficult teachers to express disapproval. The teachers reported, however, that "direct action seldom happens." They suggested that some difficult teachers are unaware of the effect that their behavior has on others. Making them aware of the inappropriateness of their behavior may resolve the problem. Teachers emphasized the importance of showing concern toward the difficult teacher, noting the expressions of frustration, unhappiness, or anger and offering an opportunity to talk. If the teacher persists with unacceptable behavior, however, teachers were emphatic about the need for the principal to pursue the issue with a behavior plan, monitoring, an offer for assistance, and consequences for noncompliance.

Administrator Attrition

Although most administrators do not abandon their positions because of problems with difficult teachers, some administrators admitted being relieved when they had opportunities to move on to another position or the teachers transferred to another school. One of them explained, "Although I moved on for other reasons, there have been one or two [teachers] that I have been relieved not to have to continue to work with." Another principal said, "If I could have (too close to retirement), I would have [left] a few years ago—I've toughened up" (Brock & Grady, 2006). One administrator did report leaving a position: "The teachers did not care about the students and would not fulfill their obligations."

TAKE ACTION!

- Take the time to consider the individual faculty members in your school. Identify the difficult teachers. Determine how their behaviors match the "Who Are They?" list on page 7.
- Remember to show concern for the difficult teachers.

CHAPTER TWO

Difficult Teachers, Difficult Behaviors

○ Naming their behaviors
○ Telling their stories

The following sections include descriptions of the motivations for common behaviors displayed by difficult teachers. Examples of how inappropriate behaviors are rewarded are described. Suggestions for removing the rewards follow these descriptions. For the sake of illustration, we depict difficult teachers in our scenarios as generally cooperative. However, bear in mind that difficult teachers want and are accustomed to getting their way. They may become angry or uncooperative in hopes that you will give in to their behavior. When that happens it is important to remain calm and steadfast in your approach and expectations.

CHRONIC COMPLAINERS

Chronic complainers find fault with a variety of aspects of the school. As one principal observed, the complainer's favorite phrase is, "Can I talk to you for a minute? . . . And then they [bring up] a thousand things." Complainers do not want to be held accountable for problems; instead, they blame others. They want someone else to solve the problems. They have an external locus of control, a sense that they are powerless to control events in their life (Bramson, 1981).

Be aware, however, that hidden among their many complaints may be a legitimate problem that needs to be addressed. Because complainers have called "wolf" too many times, their legitimate complaints tend to be overlooked.

The In-Your-Face Complainer

There are several types of complainers. One type gripes incessantly to the principal with the underlying message that the principal should be doing something to fix the problem. Their complaints are based in fact and usually reflect real problems. However, they feel helpless about solving the problem. Instead, they bring the problem to the principal, which absolves them of any responsibility: "Here is the problem; do something about it!" They also use accusations with a kernel of truth to them to avoid being held accountable for their actions (Bramson, 1981).

Consider how this complainer successfully deflects accountability, derails the conversation, and puts the principal on the defensive.

Principal Waitley: Mrs. Derailer, I noticed that you have not submitted your semester grades. They were due yesterday.

Mrs. Derailer: If we had an appropriate online form for grade recording and submission, my grades would always be timely. Our system is outdated, inadequate, and impossible to use. The time faculty wastes using this process is ridiculous. And then there's the problem of the hardware we use. I haven't had a new computer for six years, and I'm tired of having it crash all the time.

Principal Waitley: I realize that the software is cumbersome and needs to be updated. And we could use new computers, but there just isn't enough money in the budget.

Mrs. Derailer: I see money being budgeted for other things! The faculty should have input into budget priorities. . . .

In this example, the difficult teacher is "rewarded" by the principal accepting responsibility for the problem. The difficult teacher has achieved her objective. Instead of allowing the complainer to derail the conversation, keep the person and the conversation focused:

Principal Waitley: Mrs. Derailer, I noticed that you have not submitted your semester grades. They were due yesterday.

Mrs. Derailer: If we had an appropriate online form for grade recording and submission my grades would always be timely. Our system is outdated, inadequate, and impossible to use. The time faculty wastes using this process is ridiculous. And then there's the problem of the hardware we use. I haven't had a new computer for six years, and I'm tired of having it crash all the time.

Principal Waitley: I am aware of your technology concerns. However, at this time the concern is the semester grades. The grades were due yesterday, so please submit them by the end of the day.

Instead of allowing complainers to transfer problems to you, hand the problem back and move them out of their comfort zone by engaging in problem solving (Bramson, 1981). It is unlikely that one conversation will solve Mrs. Derailer's penchant for tardiness or her tactics to sidestep accountability. However, consistency in refusing to reward her behavior will lessen its frequency.

- Listen attentively to the problem.
- Keep the complainer focused on the issue.
- Paraphrase the key points of the problem as you understand them.
- Identify the problem.
- Engage the individual in problem solving by asking questions such as, "How do you think you could handle that?" "What steps could you take to solve the problem?"
- Have the complainer outline a plan of action and timeline with you.

Mr. Notfair is a frequent visitor to the principal's office. Today, his complaint is about his class. Consider how the principal, Mrs. Smylen, hands the problem back to Mr. Notfair to solve.

Mr. Notfair:	I don't think it's fair that we have so many under-achieving students in this school. Students don't turn in homework, and their parents don't care. Half of them can't even read on grade level. They're not going to pass fifth grade.
Principal Smylen:	It sounds as if you are concerned that students are not doing their homework. Exactly how many students are having that problem?
Mr. Notfair:	Probably five of them, and they're not going to pass. I keep calling their parents, but they don't care. All my work is just a waste of time. I think I'm just going to start sending them all to your office. Maybe you can straighten them out.
Principal Smylen:	Let's focus on those five students. Why do you think they are not doing their homework?
Mr. Notfair:	It's their parents' fault. Nobody cares at home. Besides, their reading levels are so low, they probably can't read the material.
Principal:	So you think their low reading level might be discouraging them from doing their home-work. What can you do about that?
Mr. Notfair:	I don't know; nothing works.
Principal Smylen:	Let's think of just one thing that might encour-age the students to do their homework.
Mr. Notfair:	Well, I could start by making the reading assignment shorter so it doesn't seem so over-whelming. But I don't think that's fair to the other kids.
Principal Smylen:	Shortening the reading assignment sounds like a good start. Let's write that down as the plan for the next two weeks. Then we will meet again to see how that is working.

In this example, Mr. Notfair is complaining but provides a suggestion for encouraging students to do their homework. However, if he is a career complainer, Mr. Notfair may not have solutions to the students' homework challenges. In that case, the principal needs to brainstorm ideas with Mr. Notfair and encourage (or ask) him to select one. The intention is to redirect him from nonproductive complaining to possible solutions.

One principal said she derailed complainers by greeting them with ". . . a smile and a compliment. If a complaint came to my ears, I asked for a written follow-up. I tell teachers that unless they write it down, I might forget it. I also refuse to respond to a complaint until I have had time to gather information." In addition, requiring that at least one suggested solution accompany every written complaint would encourage complainers to engage in problem solving and promote a solution-oriented environment.

Another principal said, "[When teachers complain,] I ask them to come up with a plan to make things equitable. I talk with them about the difference between professions and jobs, also that teachers' job responsibilities are based on student needs not teacher needs. I point out that other [teachers] face the same difficulties."

Another principal suggested, "Make it [chronic complaining] work for you." Chronic complainers enjoy complaining and are good at finding fault. Give the complainer a challenging task that uses the teacher's skills, such as chairing a task force to gather information and evaluate a school program. Be sure to balance the group with positive individuals to provide counterbalance to the faultfinder.

Some complainers are not looking for solutions; they just want someone to listen, acknowledge their feelings, and appreciate their efforts. Teachers who complain a lot might need a boost of self-esteem. One principal suggested, "Praise work the teacher has done and show appreciation." Try building the teacher's confidence by strengthening your support of the teacher's strong points. Look for specific and sincere ways to recognize and reward the teacher for doing a good job. When possible, praise the teacher in front of others, a group of parents, colleagues, or the superintendent. During social gatherings, praise the teacher in front of family members or friends.

Faculty Room Complainers

Another type of complainers haunts the faculty lounge and unloads their troubles and complaints on anyone unfortunate enough to enter. Favorite topics revolve around "lazy students," "disinterested parents," "overwhelming workload," "unfair treatment," and "the flaws of the principal." They want others to acknowledge their difficulties and offer sympathy for their plight. Although occasional complaining is a normal means of venting emotion, chronic complainers annoy others and diminish the climate of the school. The behavior tends to become so habitual that they are unaware of how frequently they complain and how much their behaviors annoy those around them. They are rewarded when other teachers listen, sympathize, and join in their complaints.

One way to deal with this type of complainers is to point out their behavior. Initiate a purposeful conversation such as, "I've noticed you complaining about your class lately. Are you unhappy with your students?" Teachers who are unaware of their complaining will be surprised that you noticed. Sometimes making them aware of the extent of their complaining or that you notice it will reduce the occurrence. If, however, they express a problem, such as "Kids today just don't behave," question them until you define a specific problem. Then engage them in solving the problem: "What can you do to improve the discipline in your class?" Have them create an action plan and timeline.

Group Complainers

A group of complainers who share a common planning time or lunch period can undermine the climate of a school. Collectively, they can become a toxic influence on teacher morale: as one teacher said, "Like a drop of poison in Camelot." Whenever possible, rearrange planning and lunch times to break up groups of complainers. One principal reported rearranging teachers' classrooms so complainers were no longer side-by-side. One principal of a large school initiated mini-faculty meetings instead of whole group meetings to disengage group complainers. The mini-faculty meetings allowed more teacher engagement in the discussion and allowed the structuring of more positive and productive meetings.

NEGATIVE TEACHERS

Negative teachers are unhappy people who are closely related to complainers. They will be the first to announce that "the idea won't work," "the new curriculum will fail," "students won't follow the new discipline code," and "parents won't cooperate." They will eagerly form a welcoming committee for new teachers and student teachers to share "what teaching is really like," "what's wrong with the school," "which students are troublemakers," "which parents are a nuisance," and "how inept the principal is." To them, the glass is always half empty. Since negative thinking can become a habit, teachers may be unaware of the frequency of their negative behavior. However, continuous negativity can also indicate an inappropriate career choice or teacher burnout (Brock & Grady, 2002).

A negative teacher or group of negative teachers can derail the successful implementation of an initiative. When new proposals are abandoned or fail, the negative teachers are rewarded. If negative teachers are not asked to participate in initiatives, they are rewarded. The negative teachers "knew" the idea would not work, and they did not want to participate in the initiative.

Negative teachers enjoy having an audience of likeminded individuals. Groups of negative teachers tend to band together and have the same demoralizing effect on school climate as complainers. Negative teachers are eager to welcome new teachers into their fold. The vulnerability of new teachers makes them prime targets for recruitment. To counter this, school leaders should assign new teachers and student teachers to teach with and share planning and lunch times with positive, collaborative teachers. Strategies to disband clusters of complainers are also critical in maintaining a positive school culture.

When confronted with negative teachers, some principals said they devoted their attention to the positive teachers and ignored those who were negative. They gave "positive reinforcement to teachers who supported an initiative." They ignored the negative teachers, continued with their plans, and let it be known that they expected everyone to participate. One principal said, "I let the negative person know that this is the direction we are going. Eventually, the negative person sees that he or she is being left behind and gets on board."

Principals reported additional strategies for working with negative teachers. These strategies included breaking old habits and assigning new responsibilities. Examples of these strategies follow:

One approach is to assign the negative teacher to work with a positive and collaborative group. "A teacher who shows early signs of negativity can be reprogrammed through positive collaborations." If the school has clusters of negative teachers, rearrange lunch schedules, planning periods, and reassign rooms to interrupt old habits, routines, and negative collaborations.

Another approach is to assign the negative teacher new or additional responsibilities and challenges. When good teachers become negative, complaining, or cynical they may be bored, disillusioned, or spiraling into burnout (Brock & Grady, 2002). They may have taught the same grade level or subject in the same room and had the same responsibilities for too long. They need new challenges—a major change—job enrichment (Herzberg, 1968). If that appears to be the case, discuss the possibilities of a change in responsibilities, a new role, or different grade level with the teacher. One principal reported an incredible transformation when a teacher moved to a different grade level. The teacher changed from a negative and cynical teacher to a positive and invigorated teacher. In some cases, a negative teacher, particularly one who is spiraling into burnout, may be revitalized by a transfer to a new school and a new beginning (Brock & Grady, 2002). Teachers who no longer enjoy teaching should be counseled into a more satisfying career choice.

INFLEXIBLE TEACHERS

Inflexible teachers want to avoid change. Like the negative teachers, they oppose new initiatives but sometimes for different reasons. Some teachers become inflexible because they are disenchanted and disillusioned after years of experiencing a steady stream of proposed change initiatives. To them, it is the "new initiative of the week," and they resent the investment of time in initiatives of short duration and uncertain outcomes. Their sentiments are, "Been there; done that; won't last; why bother?" According to one principal, "[Inflexible teachers believe] I've been around for a long time, and I've seen education go this way and that way. If I just stand still long enough, sooner or later, it will come around to my way of thinking again."

Other inflexible teachers are resistant to change because they fear how the change may affect them. After years in a comfort zone, they are uncertain of their ability to learn new information, different approaches, and advanced skills. The introduction of technology in schools precipitated many instances of teacher anxiety and difficulty in adapting to the new technology tools. Some inflexible teachers refused to use it; others, nearing retirement, left their teaching positions early. As one teacher told her principal, "I'm three or four years from retirement, why would I do that at this point?" In some schools, each new technological advance triggers another wave of resistance or refusal to adapt. One principal observed, "[I think] lazy might be a subheading under inflexible . . . sometimes teachers are inflexible because they don't want to go through the work of doing it differently."

In some instances, principals avoid implementing new programs because they dread dealing with inflexible teachers. Principals may resist assigning responsibilities to inflexible teachers because they do not want to deal with their complaints. Whenever new initiatives are discarded or leaders avoid involving a resistant teacher in a new initiative, they are rewarding and thus perpetuating inflexible behavior. The inflexible teachers get exactly what they want—the power to block change, or if the change does occur, they are not required to participate in it. Often, when change occurs, the same hardworking, cooperative teachers bear all of the responsibility for the new initiative.

The following method of initiating change is useful when dealing with inflexible teachers:

- Explain the reasons for the change.
- Listen to arguments; be honest about the obstacles and how they can be overcome.
- Cite the benefits for students.
- Help teachers see how the change will help them.
- Show them the research that supports the change.
- Give examples of other schools where the proposed change is working.
- Have teachers visit teachers from other schools that have successfully implemented the change.

- Assure teachers that they will have ample time and training to learn new skills or to implement a new program.
- Provide time and assistance for teachers to acquire new learning and skills.
- Require the participation of all teachers.
- Give the teachers ownership of the change.
- Praise progress.

Principals suggest involving resistant teachers in planning for change. Teachers who tend to resist change benefit by increased involvement in the change process. One principal said, "When making changes, I often ask [the inflexible teacher] to brainstorm with me; to help me decide how to make the change. For example, I needed to change our dismissal policy, so I asked my two inflexible teachers to help me write the policy and present it to the staff." Another principal suggested having the resistant teacher chair a major committee, "Find a part of the change that might appeal [to the teacher] and put the teacher in charge of that part."

NONCOMPLIANT TEACHERS

Noncompliant teachers want power to do things their way. They may be either aggressive or passive-aggressive. Although they behave differently, both aggressive and passive-aggressive teachers want control. You know where you stand with aggressive teachers because they tell you they cannot or will not meet your expectations. Although they are subtler, passive-aggressive teachers are more commonplace in schools than aggressive teachers are, and they are equally adept at noncompliance. They simply forget deadlines and events and arrive late for meetings. One principal reported constant frustration with a teacher who "possesses excellent teaching skills but is chronically late for meetings and deadlines." When noncompliant teachers are allowed to continue being noncompliant without penalty, they are rewarded for their behavior.

If a deadline or meeting time is established, it needs to be enforced; otherwise, your deadlines will be viewed as meaningless. Teachers who miss deadlines or arrive late at meetings should be held accountable during a conference with the principal. They should be informed of the inconvenience their tardiness creates for others. They should be made aware that a pattern of missed deadlines and late arrivals will be noted in their personnel file and considered during evaluations.

GOSSIPERS

Gossip is an old and common form of human communication. Gossip includes malicious or slanderous statements about other individuals. Researchers suggest a variety of social purposes for gossiping, including maintaining social boundaries between group members and outsiders; reaffirming norms and values of a particular group; obtaining information about another person, often for self-serving purposes; social management; moralizing; and entertainment (Ting-Tooney, 1979). In schools, however, gossip is best known as a vehicle for misinformation and rumor.

Where Did Gossiping Originate?

According to one principal, "Gossip . . . has been around as long as education has been around. . . . Everybody gossips. Parents and teachers gossip, and when principals get together, we gossip!" Most people gossip because they like being "in the know," and they like being the first person to share information. However, some gossipers may have a malicious intent. Their goal is revenge, and their intent is to damage the reputation and credibility of another person. When the intent of the gossip is revenge, individuals are rewarded when their victim's reputation, leadership, or career is damaged.

What Is the Cause of Gossiping?

Little conclusive evidence exists on the exact cause of gossiping. Some researchers suggest that gossip occurs to fill in gaps of information, indicating an absence of channels for open communication (Anderson, 1995). Most faculties include at least one "chicken little" alarmist who starts rumors of impending doom, and then basks in the resulting anxiety and mayhem.

However, gossip is integral to human socialization, sometimes used as a friendship builder especially for women who develop relationships through sharing information about themselves and

others. The intention of these gossipers is not deliberately malicious. For them, telling secrets is part of friendship. Similar sentiments were reflected on a pillow in Alice Roosevelt Longworth's
home that read, "If you can't say anything good about someone,
sit right here by me."

The Result of Gossiping

Regardless of the cause, gossip steals time, hurts morale, and
sows seeds of dissension in the workplace (Anderson. 1995). "The
problem," according to one principal, "is that gossipers have par-
tial bits of information and elaborate on them in ways that are not
productive." When information about what is happening in
school is misconstrued, gossip becomes damaging. The end result
is poor public relations. When malicious gossip occurs about
school leaders, careers are threatened and sometimes damaged.

What Do Gossipers Want?

It takes two to gossip: a talker and a listener. Gossipers are
rewarded when people listen to their tales. There are three
basic types of gossipers: the Chatterbox, the Tattler, and the
Backstabber. Although they are similar in that they want attention, their motivations are somewhat different.

Three Types of Gossipers

Chatterboxes

Chatty Cathys and Charlies reside in every school. You can recognize them by their opening line, "Have you heard?" They receive
enjoyment from being the first to know and the first to tell everyone
the news. However, they are generally decent people whose intent
is not to hurt anyone. Because of this, some principals treat gossip
lightly. As one principal observed, "A little gossip is usually harmless." A second principal reported, "I have one person who always
knows what's going on—long before me . . . although she does not
talk [negatively] about me or about other teachers."

Although the intent of the Chatty Cathys and Charlies is usually benign and may even be grounded in fact, as the information
passes from person-to-person, it often evolves into misinformation.

Each person in the gossip chain adds a nuance and omits or adds something until the message becomes unrecognizable. When this occurs, a little gossip is no longer harmless.

Principals in our studies were keenly aware that a little "harmless" gossip can quickly mushroom into a widespread problem. They acted quickly to correct misinformation and squelch the gossiping. They agreed, however, gossipers are difficult to detect and slippery to control. As one principal observed, "They are difficult to deal with because they work behind the scenes so you are not quite sure who it is, and they always deny that they've been a part of it."

Principals used two approaches to curtail gossip: addressing the whole faculty and conferring with individual gossipers. They routinely addressed their faculties on topics such as sharing information on a need-to-know basis, confidentiality, the harmful effects of gossip on schools and careers, and what constitutes professional behavior. They made it clear that they considered gossip to be negative and destructive, and that they did not want gossip occurring in the school.

When made aware of gossip, principals corrected misinformation immediately, tracked down and confronted the gossiper. Conversations with gossipers included topics such as confidentiality issues, the importance of sharing accurate information, and the damage that results from gossip. The seriousness and frequency of the gossip determined how they approached the gossiper. One principal, who reported having only one occasional gossiper, used humor to make the gossiper aware of her concern, "I gave her a hard time, and told her . . . you are the last person I will tell anything because everybody will know." For occasional or minor gossip, the principals confronted the teacher about the misinformation with a warning not to repeat the behavior. When gossiping behavior continued after a warning or did serious harm, principals documented the behavior for inclusion in the appraisal process. Although none of the principals reported terminating a teacher for gossiping, Anderson (1995) suggested that as a last resort, elimination of a gossiper might be necessary to prevent continued poisoning of the climate.

Tattletales

Although tattletales are generally considered to be children, some people continue this behavior into adulthood. By then, they have perfected their presentation style into the form of a helping hint with the opening phrase, "I just thought you should know . . ." Tattletales are gossipers who feel compelled to tell the principal about perceived misdeeds of their colleagues. Similar to children, they do not like the idea that they are playing by the rules and others are not. They parade to the office with tales such as, "I just thought you should know that Marie leaves school early every day" "Jeffrey arrives late every morning" "the kids are out of control in Mark's classroom" and "the English teachers have been criticizing your new curriculum plan behind your back."

Principals were adamant about not acting on information from tattletales and not giving them feedback. One principal reported, "I really don't believe all I . . . hear, it is demoralizing." Another principal admitted, "I must admit, [in the past] I have succumbed to listening and even acting on information gained from the gossiper. Now, I try hard to cut this person off when they start talking. If I can't, I listen, smile, and thank them for sharing. They want some kind of reaction; I try not to give feedback." Bramson (1981) suggests responding to tattletales by asking if they have talked with the person. If they have not talked with the person, which is probably the case, ask if you may use their name.

The conversation might sound like this: "I understand that you are concerned that Marie is leaving school before the contracted time. Have you mentioned this to Marie or asked her why she leaves early? You have not? Then perhaps that would be a good idea. If I talk with Marie, I will need to tell her who reported information about her. Do I have your permission to mention your name?" In the unlikely event that the tattletale gives permission, you have the option of approaching the accused and discussing the complaint. Understand, however, doing so may create hard feelings between the parties and spawn another set of problems. Consequently, the complaint should be of a serious nature before using that option. If the tattletale wants to remain confidential, say, "I cannot discuss information about any other personnel with you, and I am not comfortable talking about people who are not present. However, rest assured that when I witness inappropriate behaviors, I address them."

Backstabbers

Backstabbers, referred to as backbiters by some, are people who speak badly of someone without that person's knowledge. In person, they are polite and friendly, all the while collecting information to twist and use for their own purposes. When the person's back is turned, they spread lies to others. Teachers who are backstabbers want to discredit or embarrass someone, usually the principal. Unfortunately, they are difficult to detect until damage is done.

Women school leaders in a study by Brock (2008, July) reported being taken unaware by people whom they considered to be trusted friends and colleagues. They reported that the hurt of being betrayed by someone they trusted was often worse than the damage to their reputation. Although the backstabbing incidents they reported had occurred early in their careers, they continued to be vividly painful recollections.

Principals generally agreed that backstabbers need to be confronted as illustrated by the following comments and suggestions:

> When you find out who they are, make sure you do not make the mistake of thinking they will become loyal if you confide in them—wrong!

> If it's a minor matter, or a difference of opinion, I give grace and forgiveness and don't let it bother me. If it is more serious, I talk with the person directly (typically multiple conversations over a period of time). If I don't get anywhere, I document and see if the person might be better off employed elsewhere.

> This is hard to catch; however, if I do, it's an appraisal issue. I cite them for insubordination.

> I let them know that I am aware of their words and actions. Sometimes that changes their attitude.

> I confront them individually—"It surprised me that you said that to me and then did or said the opposite. What are you thinking, and how can we work together?"

> Let them know that trust has been broken.

A confrontation with a backstabber might sound like the following:

Principal Wise to Department Chair:	Mrs. Stabber, when we met last week, you initiated a discussion about needed changes in class schedules for your department. We agreed on what changes would be best and collaborated in rewriting the schedule. Yet, the

minutes from your department meeting indicate the opposite. You did not mention that you initiated the changes, explain why they were needed, or support them. Teachers in your department are furious that I changed schedules without input from members of the department. I trusted you to share accurate information and share responsibility for a change that you initiated. What can we do to resolve this situation?

Mrs. Stabber: I told them it was my idea, but the person recording the minutes probably didn't write that down. I don't know why they are so upset.

Principal Wise: Please schedule a meeting for tomorrow so you can correct any misinformation and answer questions. I will attend so teachers know that I am supportive of the scheduling changes that you initiated.

ANARCHISTS

The anarchist wants power. He or she wants to be in charge. The goal is to erode the principal's leadership. The tactic is to make the leader appear ineffective and thereby gain power with peers. As one principal observed, "Teachers who have a 'following' or support system within the staff can be difficult, especially if enough of the 'swing voters' go along." Some anarchists are informal leaders who become disenchanted with the leader's decisions. Others are frustrated leaders or "wannabe" principals who think they can do a better job of running a school.

Leadership change in a school can be a catalyst for anarchy. When a new administrator is hired, conditions are optimal for anarchists to emerge, especially if the following conditions exist:

- The school has had a rapid turnover of administration, allowing individuals to seize informal leadership.
- Teachers have strong loyalties to the departing principal.

- An informal leader in the school was one of the applicants for the administrator's position. (Brock & Grady, 1995)

New administrators need to investigate the succession issues that surround their hiring. If one or more of these conditions exist, the new administrator should be prepared for a possible power struggle with an anarchist. In an effort to sabotage the administrator's efforts, the anarchist will ignore directives, withhold critical information, belittle the leader, and recruit followers among the faculty and parents. Some anarchists use hidden tactics such as backstabbing and withholding critical pieces of information as their weapons of sabotage. Others, however, display overt dissension, engaging in loud criticism and sniping during meetings. Regardless of their tactics, their goal is to gain a willing group of followers, and ultimately have things done their way.

Confronting an anarchist head on is not always the best strategy, especially for a new principal who has yet to gain credibility with the school staff. A better choice is winning the support of the anarchist's constituents and redirecting the leadership ability of the anarchist. Principals offered the following advice:

I try to include teachers' input on decisions and to be open to suggestions. This eliminates 99% of the anarchist's activities. If it is set up right, the anarchist doesn't get followers and runs out of steam . . . [ending up] alone.

Enlist staff in all decisions effecting instructional practice, routines, and school procedures. "Our way" becomes the majority, and noisemakers, anarchists, and martyrs have no audience.

Some anarchists are frustrated leaders who will welcome an opportunity to exercise their leadership ability. Offer them the right challenge, and they may become positive leaders.

. . . if the teacher [anarchist] . . . wants power, it is usually because they fear losing control. I find that putting these people in charge helps to diffuse their fear of losing control. [For example,] one year I had a teacher who tried to change everything the Christmas play director did. The next year, I assigned the "anarchist" to be the play director.

SNIPERS

There are several motivations for sniping. According to Brickman & Kirschner (2002), people snipe when they have a grudge against someone, when they are angry over an outcome that did not go their way, or when they seek to undermine the credibility of someone. Not all sniping has a malicious intent. A few snipers are misguided jokesters out to create some laughs but who inadvertently cause hurt feelings. Sniping can also be a sign of affection between close friends who engage in an ongoing teasing banter. In a similar fashion, teachers sometimes show affection by teasing an administrator they like. The best response in that situation is to be good-natured and laugh.

When the motivation is malicious, snipers revel in the attention they gain by flustering someone. One principal said, "Outspoken behavior at a faculty meeting is difficult—it often catches the administrator off guard . . . it's undermining. Teacher snipers who are out for revenge or want to undermine an administrator's credibility make snide comments, roll their eyes, and ask questions designed to embarrass the speaker. Sometimes they disguise their true motivation by using dry humor or sarcasm. They revel in the attention of those listening and relish the damage they do to the speakers' effectiveness and credibility. The following is an example.

Sara, who was an assistant principal in the school for three years, applied for the principal's position but did not obtain it. Instead, Jane, who had only one year of experience as an assistant principal, was hired from outside the district. Sara is furious and determined to exact revenge. At every faculty meeting, she sits with her faithful followers and takes pot-shots at Jane. She makes barely audible comments and rolls her eyes, causing her friends to giggle and cover their faces. Now and then, Sara interrupts Jane with a rude comment or question. The rest of the faculty members appear uncomfortable. Jane has difficulty maintaining her train of thought and remaining composed. She is in a quandary about how to deal with Sara the Sniper.

When dealing with snipers, rule number one is to play it cool. Do not engage in a sniping contest, lash out verbally, or lose your temper. If you do, the sniper succeeds in making you look foolish and inept. One administrator likened this behavior to "Getting into a hissing contest with a snake . . . the snake always wins." Instead, think of the sniper as someone who is insecure and grasping at straws—an adult version of a naughty sixth grader—and you are the adult in control. Continue what you are saying and nonchalantly walk toward the sniper, get in her space (unless she is hiding in the back of the room), and make her uncomfortable. Do not reward her by paying attention to her or responding to her rude remarks. Instead, address your attention and responses to the rest of the faculty.

After the meeting make an appointment for a private conversation with the sniper. Inform her that her comments during the faculty meeting were inappropriate, nonproductive, and caused discomfort to the rest of the faculty. Ask her what is troubling her and how you can work together. At the end of the conversation, clearly state the behavior that you expect in the future.

Principal Stopher: Sara, during yesterday's faculty meeting, I was distracted by the comments and gestures you were making to your friends while I was talking. The rest of the faculty seemed uncomfortable and embarrassed by your comments. Did you have a problem with something I was saying?

Sara the Sniper: I didn't mean anything; I was just joking around.

Principal Stopher: I see. Well, in the future, I would appreciate it if you refrained from "joking around" while I am talking. Your input and questions are always welcome. However, I prefer that you share them with the entire group.

BULLIES

According to one principal, "There are two kinds of bullies: those who use intimidation in the faculty lounge and those who use it in the classroom." Intimidators want power and are rewarded when they get their way. Teachers who are intimidators in meetings and the faculty lounge think they know what is right and what should happen. They have no patience with discussion, little regard for the feelings and ideas of others, and use intimidation as a ploy to get their message across. One principal observed, ". . . they can be very likable people. But if you hit one of their hot-button issues, it's boom! Their ears go weak, and their mouths just don't stop."

Even worse, some intimidators extend their bullying to the classroom where they become teacher tyrants. Their classrooms are run like miniature fiefdoms in which they are the master and the students are the serfs who live in fear of displeasing them. Rules and consequences for misbehavior are written in concrete. Students who make a mistake, misbehave, or dare to challenge their authority receive swift and harsh punishment. Administrators are usually alerted to the presence of a teacher tyrant by numerous parental complaints and conflicts with students. As one principal explained, "[I know I have a teacher tyrant] if enough students tell me that [the teacher] loses his temper, uses a voice that is too loud, and is intimidating . . . and then the parents repeat the same thing. You know the old adage, If it walks like a duck, quacks like a duck, it must be a duck!"

Bullies are rewarded when people acquiesce to them. To stop bullying and intimidation, stop the reward. The principal needs to let the intimidator and the entire faculty know that the discussion will continue and the decision will be made after everyone is heard. The following is an example of how the faculty discussion would sound:

Irene the Intimidator:	That will never work, Tom. I've already told you we should. . . .
Principal:	Irene, you have shared several good ideas. However, we need to hear from everyone. Tom, I am interested in hearing your idea. Please elaborate on your suggestion.
Principal:	Thank you, Tom. Now let's hear from everyone else. Mary, what do you think . . . ?

If a pattern of intimidation has been firmly entrenched and people are reluctant to speak, the principal may need to establish ground rules for discussions, such as listening respectfully, encouraging everyone to contribute, and acknowledging the merit of others' contributions. Reluctance to speak can be overcome by asking everyone to write down ideas or suggestions at the beginning of the meeting. Collect them and call on each person to elaborate on his or her idea or suggestion. As one principal said, "Give strong support to each person" to help teachers stand up to the intimidator. Once teachers are able to stand up to the intimidator, the behavior usually disappears.

After the meeting, arrange a private conference with Irene, the Intimidator. As one principal advised, ". . . use a mild demeanor [and meet] in a private place so you don't back a bully into a corner." Use the example from the meeting to explain to the Intimidator how her comment was hurtful to Tom and inhibited others from sharing. She may be unaware of how others perceive her. Encourage her to continue sharing ideas but also to be receptive and respectful when others contribute. Discuss the importance of teamwork.

Students should never be expected to put up with a teacher who treats them with disrespect. Teachers who engage in bullying or intimidation need to be informed that their behavior is inappropriate and placed on improvement plans in accordance with school district policies.

Principals offered the following examples of incidents that contributed to their decisions:

> The teacher lied about making inappropriate comments to students, was negative with students and peers, and grabbed a student during a behavior confrontation.

> He lost his temper easily with students and peers, was overly emotional with students, picked on several students, humiliated students, and shared documentation from me [about his behavior] with some of his students.

> The teacher used sarcasm.

> The teacher made negative comments and intimidated students. One day a student failed to put her name on her paper. The teacher picked up the paper, wadded it up in front of the class, and threw it in the trash. That was the last straw.

> The teacher persisted in inappropriate and punitive treatment of students.

> The teacher failed to change behaviors even after mentoring, discussion, and help were provided.

When a teacher does not respond to improvement plans and persists in bullying, intimidating, or other inappropriate behavior with students, the principal must present the documentation of the teacher's behavior to the superintendent. The superintendent, then, must determine if the documentation should be presented to the school board according to district policies and procedures.

NOISEMAKERS

Noisemakers feel "wronged" in some respect and want the attention of the media, school board, parents, and whoever will listen to their tale of woe. They want others to acknowledge their plight, affirm their injury, and join them in seeking revenge against the principal. They are rewarded when others listen to their story and support them.

Difficult teachers who are vocal—such as anarchists, snipers, gossipers, and complainers—sometimes become noisemakers when they are counseled to improve their behavior or placed on improvement plans. When a difficult teacher is terminated, it is not unusual for their followers to develop into a posse of noisemakers who protest the unjust decision. This is a difficult situation for administrators who are unable to justify their actions due to the confidentiality of personnel issues.

When noisemaking occurs because a teacher is displeased with an administrator's decisions, the administrator has the following options. Some administrators met with the disgruntled teacher and listened to concerns.

I sit down with them and discuss the perspectives of everyone involved.

I ask, "How would you like to see things handled or done?"

I ask them to come to me first with concerns; I listen to their perspective and explain why I am doing something.

I go to the teacher personally—often they just want to be heard. I ask them to explain and clarify their concerns.

Other administrators reminded noisemakers of the policy related to speaking to the media and the negative impact of their noisemaking:

I reinforce the district policy on who in the district will speak to the media. I reinforce the chain of command and district procedures. I remind them that this issue is included in teacher evaluations.

I share the negative impact of noisemaking on them personally and on the school.

I remind them they have an obligation to the school to solve this in an agreeable manner.

I ask if what they are doing is in the best interest of the students and the district.

A few of the administrators opted for the riskier approach of calling the noisemaker's bluff. They challenged noisemakers to "go for it" but warned them of the consequences of doing so.

I tell them to go for it. I always try to have my ducks in a row so I can call their bluff.

I generally say that [talking to the media, school board] is their right and privilege, but it can cut both ways. I remind them that all the facts are likely to come out, not just the ones that are supportive of their view. I'm never afraid to answer to the board if I've been doing my job.

I let them make noise. I even offer them the phone number. I always inform the superintendent—warn him of impending doom.

I challenge them—sometimes you can call their bluff.

As tempting as it may be to challenge a noisemaker, calling the teacher's bluff might not work. If the noisemaker persists, damage to the school, the administrator, and even the noisemaker's reputation could occur. Left unresolved, the conflict may continue to fester causing additional problems among the staff.

A safer option for dealing with a noisemaker is to meet with the individual, listen to concerns, and explain your actions. If the matter is confidential, explain the confidentiality issue. If you cannot come to a resolution, remind the noisemaker of the school policy for expressing dissent and speaking with the media, and the consequences of nonadherence to school policy. Although teachers do have rights to express their opinion, they need to do so in a professional manner and in accordance with school policy.

SELFISH TEACHERS

Selfish teachers have a nine-to-five job mentality and want to avoid working any more than necessary. It is all about them—not the students. To them teaching is a "job" to which they intend to devote as little time as possible. One administrator described them as, "Stingy with time when everyone else does a lot more than is required." Another administrator observed, "They do not understand the big picture; they are self-centered." They commit the terms of their contract to memory and at any given moment can quote the requirements stated therein. Volunteering is not an option.

Because selfish teachers are so unwilling and make such a fuss when asked to exert any extra effort, principals seldom ask them to assume any challenging responsibilities or difficult classes. By doing so, principals reward them with exactly what they want—as little work as possible. A better choice is assigning and holding selfish teachers accountable for the same number of assignments and duties as everyone else.

TAKE ACTION!

- Develop descriptions of the difficult teachers you identified at the end of Chapter 1.
- Identify ways they have impeded the development of a team spirit in the school.
- Provide a list of the actions you have taken in the past to address their difficult behaviors.

Part II

Solutions and Strategies

Facilitating Behavior Change

Conversations, Warnings,
and Improvement Plans

People don't resist change. They resist being changed!

—Peter Senge

○ Establish rapport before a problem occurs

○ Visit classrooms

○ Start with a purposeful conversation

○ Follow up with a verbal warning

○ Adhere to district policies and procedures

BEFORE A PROBLEM OCCURS

Establishing rapport with individual teachers is a critical first step in curtailing and preventing difficult behaviors and developing effective teams. Teachers who feel respected and valued by the principal are less likely to engage in difficult behavior. Principals gain rapport, trust, and respect by establishing personal relationships with each teacher. Part of each day should be spent engaging in conversations with individual teachers. When and if the need arises for a conversation about inappropriate behavior, the principal has the advantage of a previously established basis of trust. Additionally, personal knowledge about the teacher provides a greater understanding of issues and motivations that may contribute to inappropriate behavior.

Establishing a pattern for routine classroom visits is equally important. Teachers who know that you will drop in for brief visits will be more aware of their behavior toward students. Also, if you routinely visit classrooms, you will have a more accurate sense of what is occurring in the building. Teachers whose behavior you are monitoring will feel less conspicuous among their peers. One principal made a practice of making brief visits of five minutes or less to at least six classrooms every day. She carried a notebook and kept a log of what she observed at each stop. Every week, she visited each of the thirty classrooms in her building at least once or more. By varying the order of the visits and the time of day, teachers and students had no idea when she would visit.

At each stop, she jotted down a positive observation and left a note in the teacher's mailbox. If something disturbed her or if she had a question, she visited with the teacher at the end of the day.

There is no "one way" to handle everyone who displays difficult behavior. When confronted with a difficult person, we have several options. If the behavior is merely annoying to us and causes no real damage, we can ignore it, change our attitude, and laugh it off or learn to put up with it. If, however, the behavior is continuous and bothersome to a wide range of people and causes disruption and potential damage, we need to change our response to the person, thereby influencing a behavior change. If the behavior is psychologically or physically threatening or damaging to us or others, the best choice is to remove ourselves or the person from the situation.

Your Attitude Is Important

Your attitude toward the origins of difficult behavior has an influence on your success in influencing behavior change. Think of difficult behavior as a learned response. Regarding difficult behavior as a learned response suggests the possibility that the behavior can be changed. By contrast, labeling someone as having a difficult personality suggests that the person cannot change. Most of the principals in our studies identified the cause of difficult behavior as learned, suggesting that old behaviors can be modified and new behaviors learned. One principal noted that difficult behaviors were often the result of "behaviors accepted where they were before." Other principals explained,

> Much of it is the result of their experiences as a student, teacher, and what is learned from other staff. Sometimes it is a result of family and home [experiences].

> [It's] learned behavior [that] meets their needs. If I seek attention and the only way to do that is by complaining or gossiping, that's what I'll do, if no other need-meeting skills are developed.

A few of the principals in our studies attributed difficult behavior to a teacher's personality or "just plain genes" rather than identifying a specific behavior problem. One reported, "Most of my teacher problems have been [caused by] personality." The principal noted, "Personality . . . is difficult to change."

Labeling teachers as "personality problems" removes any hope of influencing a change. Some of the principals in our studies identified difficult teachers as being unhappy and bitter, feeling unsuccessful, lacking in self-confidence, and having self-esteem problems. Although these may be accurate descriptions of how difficult teachers feel, these labels are not helpful in identifying and solving the underlying behavior problem. A better choice is to identify specific observable behaviors and change our responses to the individual.

Understand the Motivation

Before we can influence behavior change, we need to separate the person from the behavior. Separating the person from the behavior helps us to shape an objective view of the problem and formulate an appropriate response. Detach emotionally and try to understand the viewpoint of the difficult person. Getting to know someone can change your attitude and provide information that will increase your ability to work with the person. Consider the possibility that the teacher may seem difficult to you because you approach problems and situations differently. For instance, some individuals prefer to eliminate lengthy discussion, make quick decisions, and get the job done in as short a time as possible. A more reflective individual prefers time to think through situations and discuss options.

All behavior is chosen on some level and serves a purpose for an individual. The most common motivators for human behavior include a desire for attention, power, avoidance, revenge, or learned helplessness. Understanding the difficult person you are working with is essential. Listen carefully to what the teacher says and does, the circumstances surrounding the unwanted behavior, and how you and others respond. Does the teacher feel misunderstood, overwhelmed, unappreciated, threatened by change, or bored with work? Does the teacher need additional challenges, leadership opportunities, or simply more input into decisions? Does the teacher resent or harbor jealousy toward you? Finding out what motivates a difficult teacher can change the dynamics of the relationship. Greater understanding may enable you to transform a difficult teacher into a positive addition to the faculty.

Why do some principals manage difficult teachers better than others? They know what actions to take to level the balance of power and how to minimize the impact of difficult behavior in their organization (Bramson, 1981). Some leaders have learned a repertoire of verbal skills to contend with problem behaviors. However, few leaders are actually aware of the strategies they use (Kosmoski & Pollack, 2000) and are thus unable to replicate them or describe them. To increase the information available to principals, we conducted studies of the strategies used by veteran principals to address difficult behavior. The following sections reflect these strategies.

Ignore the Behavior

If the behavior is merely annoying and causes no real damage, ignore the behavior or learn to put up with it. Difficult behavior is in the "eye of the beholder." Sometimes a behavior that is annoying to you is not annoying to anyone else.

For instance, you know that Mrs. Branson will stop by your office to complain about her workload each time you place a new student in her class. She is an excellent teacher and just requires additional reinforcement from time to time. After you commend her for her fine teaching, she is satisfied and cooperative.

Keep in mind, however, that behavior should not be ignored merely to avoid a confrontation. Ignoring difficult behavior that disturbs you can cause feelings of resentment on your part and encourage continuation of a teacher's difficult behavior. For example, if Mrs. Branson continues to complain about new students, unfair treatment, and how hard she works on a regular basis, ignoring the behavior is not a good choice.

Change Your Attitude

Getting to know someone helps you to understand the individual's perspective and motivation. This information will improve your ability to work with the individual. Sometimes annoyances occur because people approach situations and problems differently. Instead of being difficult, the teacher's behavior might simply be different than yours.

For example, you may inherit a teacher whose behavior in and out of the classroom is playful, mischievous, and unpredictable. At first impression, the behavior seems outrageous and unacceptable. After closer examination, however, it is apparent that the teacher is an enthusiastic teacher with a big heart and a great sense of humor. This teacher thinks life and school should be fun. Students love the teacher—to the point of not wanting to stay home sick because they are afraid they will miss something. Meetings are never dull when this teacher is around! Getting to know the teacher causes your attitude to change. You may realize how much you enjoy the teacher's playful personality. You also may realize what a treasure this teacher is in the school.

Tackle the Problem

Action Is Imperative When

- The behavior damages the well-being of students.
- The behavior impedes student learning.
- The behavior destroys faculty morale.
- The behavior impedes teamwork.
- The behavior obstructs attainment of school goals.
- The behavior is psychologically or physically threatening to students or staff.

If a teacher's negative or disruptive behavior is persistent and threatens any aspect of the educational environment, the principal must resolve the problem. If you can answer yes to any of the following questions, action is imperative.

- Is this behavior damaging to the well-being of students?
- Is this behavior damaging to student learning?
- Is this behavior damaging to school climate or faculty morale?

- Is this behavior interfering with teamwork?
- Is this behavior interfering with the attainment of school goals?
- Is this behavior psychologically or physically threatening to anyone in the school community?
- Is this behavior damaging to your or anyone else's reputation and career?

HOW TO ENCOURAGE BEHAVIOR CHANGE

Most authors agree that although you cannot change another person's behavior, you can communicate with that person in a way that encourages the person to change (Bell & Smith, 2004; Brinkman & Kirschner, 2002; Gill, 1999; Podestra & Sanderson, 1999). In other words, you have to change your attitude and your behavior. You cannot change how a teacher behaves, but you can change how you respond to the behavior. By changing your behavior, you can remove the reward for the inappropriate behavior. When the inappropriate behavior is no longer rewarded, the teacher will be encouraged to change behaviors. Keep in mind that a learned behavior does not change overnight. In fact, when you change your response, the teacher may become angry or upset, and the behavior might worsen for a while. You will need to be consistent and steadfast in your response.

> To stop a behavior, extinguish the payoff the person receives for the behavior.

Be objective and nonemotional when dealing with a difficult teacher. Although it is human to feel hurt, disappointed, discouraged, or even angry when confronted by an adult behaving inappropriately, acting on those emotions will only escalate the problem. A better choice is to examine the behavior as a problem to be solved and explore possible solutions. A first step is performing an objective analysis of the current situation, past responses, and then identifying a new response. The following questions may assist you in analyzing a behavior problem and strategizing a change.

1. What specific behaviors do you want changed? Begin by identifying a behavior that can be observed rather than labeling the person. For example, "I want Teacher A to stop making cutting comments to others during faculty meetings.

His behavior is intimidating others from contributing to discussions." This is a specific behavior that can be observed and discussed with the individual.

2. What new behaviors do you want to see? For example, Teacher A should listen quietly and respectfully without interrupting. Teacher A should acknowledge the contributions of others before adding his suggestions.

3. What is motivating the teacher's undesirable behavior? The need for attention, power/control, revenge, appreciation, or recognition may precipitate the behavior. Every human behavior is chosen as an attempt to fulfill a need or want. In the example, Teacher A wants power. He thinks he knows what is best and wants to do it his way.

4. What reward is the teacher receiving for the inappropriate behavior? If you stop the reward, you can extinguish the behavior. In the example, Teacher A's nonverbal and verbal behavior stops discussion. Things are done his way— which is what he wants.

5. How have you responded in the past to the undesirable behavior? What were the outcomes? If past efforts failed, it is time to try something different. For instance, if you ignored Teacher A's intimidating behavior in the past and the behavior is continuing, clearly you need to select a different response.

6. Are there factors in the school environment that may be contributing to the behavior? Working conditions such as cleanliness, organization, school discipline, safety, and availability of resources all contribute to staff morale and individual teacher satisfaction. School subcultures are additional factors in satisfaction levels. Are your school subcultures collegial and energetic, or are they toxic denizens of malcontent? If other factors exist, you may need to look at the broader picture and make major school changes. In the example, Teacher A might be a strong informal leader among the faculty; not because he is liked—but because he is feared. If that is the case, it will take time and encouragement for teachers to regain enough confidence to speak up during meetings.

A template for developing a behavior change plan follows on page 58 and on page 144 in the Resources section.

Behavior Change Plan

The objectionable behavior: _____

The reward for the behavior: _____

The targeted new behavior: _____

Past strategies: _____

The new strategy: _____

Using the example of Teacher A, the Behavior Change Plan would look like this:

Behavior Change Plan for Teacher A

The objectionable behavior: Teacher A intimidates others by rolling his eyes, interrupting them when they are talking, and telling them that their ideas are stupid.

The reward for the behavior: Teacher A wants power and wants to do things his way.

The targeted new behavior: Teacher A should listen without interrupting. Teacher A should acknowledge the contributions of others before making suggestions.

My past response: My past response has been to ignore him. This response has only served to intensify his behavior.

My new strategy: I will meet privately with Teacher A and inform him that his behavior is intimidating others and limiting discussion during faculty meetings.

I will tell him that I want him to listen respectfully without interrupting as others speak and acknowledge their ideas and contributions before sharing his ideas and suggestions. I will share the example that occurred at the last meeting during which he rolled his eyes as Marie was offering a suggestion, interrupted her before she finished, and told her, "That's a stupid idea." The discussion ended because nobody else was willing to contribute.

When a Meeting Is Necessary

The goals of a remediation meeting are (a) to identify strategies to help the teacher understand that a behavior problem exists and (b) to correct the inappropriate behavior. Meetings should be conducted in a nonconfrontational manner and at a time when both parties are relaxed. Scheduling a meeting when one or both parties are angry or frustrated is counterproductive.

The extent of the remediation process will vary according to the nature and seriousness of the teacher's behavior problem. The procedures you use must adhere to district policies and procedures. The following strategies may be useful.

Strategies for Dealing With Difficult Teachers

Plan A: Remediate the Problem

- Step 1: The Purposeful Conversation
- Step 2: The Verbal Warning With a Letter to the Personnel File
- Step 3: The Improvement Plan Using District Procedures

Plan B: Remove the Problem

- Option 1: Teacher Transfer to a More Appropriate Setting
- Option 2: Facilitate Career Change for Teacher
- Option 3: Terminate or Nonrenewal of Contract

Plan C: Leave the Problem

Remediating the Problem

When dealing with a difficult teacher, the first step is to present your concerns and identify your expectations. Difficult behaviors must be confronted directly. As uncomfortable as this may be, presenting your concerns to the teacher is essential.

Feedback is an important tool used to provide specific information to teachers on how their behaviors are affecting the workplace (Schermerhorn, Hunt, & Osborn, 2008). Ideally, feedback should include factual information based on your observations and emotional information based on your or other peoples' reactions to the teacher's behavior (Aldrich, 2002). Objective feedback does not include value judgments or labels but rather includes specific, factual information for the teacher's consideration (Glickman, Gordon, & Ross-Gordon, 2005).

The Purposeful Conversation

The first step in dealing with difficult teachers is having a purposeful conversation to present feedback to the teacher. Some teachers are not aware of their behaviors and the effects of their behaviors on others (Scott, 2004; Stone, Patton, & Heen, 1999). Additionally, they might not be aware of the limiting effects of their behaviors on their career potential. Share your concerns by describing specific, observable behaviors and the reactions the behaviors cause. Some difficult teachers are shocked at the effects of their behaviors and make immediate changes. Other difficult teachers need more convincing. In either case, the purposeful conversation, accompanied by appropriate documentation, is an effective and positive means of initiating the process. The following steps may be a useful model:

- Present the facts.
- Allow the teacher an opportunity to respond.
- State expectations for behavior.
- Listen to the teacher's response.
- Offer assistance.
- Establish a follow-up meeting.
- Monitor performance.
- Meet and offer feedback.

Consider the following examples:

Example 1: The Venter

For the third consecutive day, Principal Schmitz hears Mr. Venter, an experienced high school math teacher, in the hallway complaining to colleagues about his classes. This year for the first time, Mr. Venter voiced several complaints about students to Principal Schmitz. Principal Schmitz has a meeting with Mr. Venter.

Principal Schmitz: How is the year going for you?

Mr. Venter: It's been a tough one.

Principal Schmitz: I have heard you complaining about your class in the hallway lately. And you have complained more than usual to me about students. Are you having problems with this group?

Mr. Venter: Well, they are a challenging bunch of kids. This has been a very difficult year for me.

Principal Schmitz:	What seems to be the problem?
Mr. Venter:	It's just that so many students have such low academic levels, and there are several ADHD kids in my classes. A lot of them are not turning in homework. Many of these kids have pretty unstable situations at home, so I'm not getting a lot of support from parents.
Principal Schmitz:	It sounds as if the low academics and behavior problems have been overwhelming for you.
Mr. Venter:	No. I think I've handled it okay. I just feel frustrated sometimes, wish I could do more. I guess I just need to tell someone how tough it is.
Principal Schmitz:	Telling people does help. Venting is a stress reliever that most of us engage in. However, when we vent in the school hallways, it can create a negative atmosphere for other people.
Mr. Venter:	I guess so. I didn't realize how noticeable it was to others.
Principal Schmitz:	I know this group is a tough bunch, but you have done wonders with them academically. Their test scores in math are higher than they ever have been. All things considered, I think you should be bragging about your success instead of complaining.
Mr. Venter:	You're right. It's easy to get bogged down in the day-to-day and forget about the big picture. They have grown a lot. I need to focus on the positive.
Principal Schmitz:	That's the spirit. Let's keep it positive.

In this case, the teacher was venting to relieve stress and was unaware of the frequency or negative overtones of the message. The principal found something genuine and specific to appreciate and commented on it to let the teacher know the value of his contributions. He also acknowledged the challenges the teacher faced.

Acknowledgement of hard work, a discussion of the importance of maintaining a positive school climate, and encouragement to speak positively in public places may be all that is needed. When teachers know you want to understand their concerns and you value their opinions, it will increase their willingness to cooperate (Lawrence, 2005).

Additionally, during conversations with complainers, you may acquire information that will enable you to meet their needs in a positive manner. For example, a complainer may have had the same responsibilities for years and be interested in a new challenge, a new grade level, a different classroom, or even a transfer to a different school. In the next example, the teacher is a chronic complainer who will likely be a "regular" in your office.

Example 2: The Chronic Complainer

Miss Complainer, a fifth-grade teacher, is a frequent visitor to Principal Wearies' office. She haunts the faculty room complaining to anyone who will listen. Principal Wearies invites her for a purposeful conversation.

Principal Wearies: How is the year going for you?

Miss Complainer: It's been just terrible.

Principal Wearies: I am sorry to hear that. I heard you complaining about your class in the faculty room this week. And last week, you voiced several complaints to me about students. What seems to be the problem?

Miss Complainer: There are too many kids with low academic levels and behavior problems in my class. It isn't fair. Why do we have to have all the low kids in this school?

Principal Wearies: We have no control over who enrolls in the school. Our job is to teach all of the students who come here. Students with lower academic levels are fairly distributed among teachers. Are you dissatisfied teaching here?

Miss Complainer: It's not that. I like teaching here. But these kids need a lot of help. It doesn't seem as if I accomplish anything, and I get so frustrated.

Principal Wearies: I know that your class started the year with some low test scores and several behavior problems, but look at the successes in the class. The students have made great improvements since the beginning of the year. You'll be more satisfied with your efforts if you focus on the successes.

Miss Complainer: I guess I have helped some of them. I understand your point about searching for successes. But I am sick and tired of parents who don't make their kid do their homework. No wonder the kids don't learn.

Principal Wearies: I know you take your job very seriously, but you need to keep a positive outlook. I'm counting on you to help me maintain the positive climate in the school.

Don't expect Miss Complainer to be "cured" by one visit. She will probably be a frequent visitor who requires ongoing encouragement and assurance that she is doing a good job. If, however, Miss Complainer is unwilling to correct her negative behavior and contributes to low morale, she may become a candidate for a performance improvement plan to get her back on track.

WHEN CONVERSATIONS FAIL

Most school districts have clear policies and procedures for handling staff misconduct. Additional resources for handling staff misconduct include *How to Handle Staff Misconduct* (Lawrence & Vachon, 2003) and *The Marginal Teacher* (Lawrence, 2005). Before launching an improvement plan, supervisors should be (a) aware of district policies and procedures for handling staff misconduct, (b) knowledgeable about state statutes relative to staff misconduct, and (c) understand the provisions of teacher contracts. A series of steps for handling misconduct may include oral reprimands, a misconduct meeting, a letter of reprimand, suspension without pay, and recommendations for termination (Lawrence & Vachon, 2003). Supervisors should be scrupulous in their adherence to district policies and procedures. Principals must follow the steps required by these policies and procedures, including informing and involving other district administrators and legal counsel in the process as required. The following examples present teachers whose behavior may signal the need for a formal improvement plan.

Example 3: Negative Outbursts

Mr. Negative interjects negative comments when you are explaining district initiatives during faculty meetings. You had several meeting to discuss the outbursts with Mr. Negative, hoping that he would cease and desist. However, he continues to complain loudly about the initiatives during and after every meeting. Since Mr. Negative is unwilling to change his behavior, you meet with Mr. Negative and give him a formal warning:

1. Describe the objectionable behavior and its effects: "Mr. Negative, the initiatives we are discussing are required by the district. Whether we agree or not does not change the necessity of our meeting district goals by the end of the year. I need everybody on board to do so. Your continued complaining creates a negative tone to the meeting, causes needless dissent, and threatens the goal attainment."

2. Describe the target behavior: "I want you to stop making critical comments about the initiative and start making positive, constructive contributions during the meetings."

3. Listen to the teacher's response.

4. Offer assistance: "Do you need assistance in making these improvements?"

5. Establish a timeline: "I will be monitoring your contributions at meetings and evaluating your progress at the end of the month."

6. Listen to the teacher's remarks.

7. Summarize what was discussed.

8. Prepare a written summary of the meeting. Give a copy to the teacher and place a copy in the file.

9. Monitor the teacher's behavior.

10. Evaluate the teacher's behavior at the end of the time period.

11. Determine the next steps. If Mr. Negative ceases his negative outbursts, no additional steps are required.

Example 4: Teacher Outburst

The supervisor meets with Mrs. Outburst, a high school English teacher, after a drop-in visit to her class.

Principal Gordon: When I dropped by your classroom this morning, I was surprised when you told Alice, "You just won the prize for today's dumbest question! I've already explained that at least ten times, but since you were too busy flirting with Tom . . . ." Alice was embarrassed, and the class looked shocked.

Mrs. Outburst: I am so embarrassed and so sorry. I have not been feeling well, and Alice has tried my patience all week. She doesn't listen; instead she spends most of class trying to get her friend, Tom's, attention. I lost my temper. I need to apologize to her.

Principal Gordon: An apology sounds like a good idea. I understand how frustrating students can be, especially when you are not feeling well. I am confident that future corrections will be handled in private and in a respectful manner.

Principal Gordon: Alice, you mentioned that you are not feeling well. Do you need to take some sick days?

Mrs. Outburst: No, I just had a touch of flu. I'm feeling better now.

Principal Gordon: I'll stop by to visit again at the end of the week.

Sometimes teachers like Mrs. Outburst do not realize how impatient or sarcastic they sound. They may not be aware that their tone of voice is becoming sarcastic, impatient, or harsh. A frustrating class, ongoing discipline problems, illness, problems at home, or the intersections of multiple issues may be contributing factors. The teacher's behavior is clearly a serious concern and should not be tolerated. If the behavior is addressed immediately, giving feedback on what was heard or observed might be all that is required for a reality check and a behavior change. Additionally, a purposeful conversation may reveal additional concerns that are affecting performance and need to be addressed.

However, if Mrs. Outburst is a teacher who routinely bullies and intimidates students, the behavior may be entrenched. She will not appreciate your criticism, and will probably respond with defiance and hostility, as illustrated in the following conversation:

Principal Gordon: When I dropped by your classroom this morning, I was surprised when you told Alice, "You just won the prize for today's dumbest question! I've already explained that at least ten times, but since you were too busy flirting with Tom . . . ." Alice was embarrassed, and the class looked shocked.

Mrs. Outburst: You should have to put up with these brats! And Alice is the worst of them. She spends all her time talking and flirting with Tom, then she has the nerve to ask a stupid question. She makes no effort and then expects me to help her. I am sick and tired of dealing with her.

Principal Gordon: I understand how frustrating some students can be. However, in this school, we speak to students in a respectful manner. Next time you need to correct a student, I want you to do so privately and use a courteous tone of voice.

Mrs. Outburst: Humph. . . . [Rolls her eyes]

Principal Gordon: You seem frustrated with your class and Alice in particular. What can you do to change your behavior? Is there anything I can do to help?

Mrs. Outburst:	I've been teaching for 20 years—I know what I'm doing. The kids are the ones with the problem.
Principal Gordon:	Treating students with respect is essential for employment in this school. I will assume that in the future you will speak to all students in a respectful tone and courteous manner. I will stop by your class on a weekly basis to see how things are going. If you need assistance, I am here to work with you.

The nature of Mrs. Outburst's response indicates that this purposeful conversation is unlikely to influence her proclivity for intimidation. Since most school districts have zero tolerance for teachers who are verbally abusive to students, Mrs. Outburst may become a candidate for an improvement plan. If that seems likely, it is imperative to know and follow district policies and procedures as you initiate the process.

Time for a Change

When a teacher's behavior is serious, violates approved district conduct policies, and an improvement plan has not been effective, it may be necessary to remove the teacher. Several possibilities for removal exist, including a transfer to a more suitable school, counseling for a career change, contract nonrenewal, or termination. As previously noted, scrupulous attention must be given to district policies and procedures and contractual agreements before taking steps to remove a teacher.

Transfers

Transferring a difficult teacher for the purpose of handing off the problem to someone else is not an appropriate solution. A transfer should occur only when a change of school environment or different leadership would elicit more appropriate behavior from the teacher. A transfer is beneficial when a personality conflict exists between the principal and teacher, between teachers, when the teacher shows signs of burnout and would benefit from a change (Brock & Grady, 2002), or when a teacher has been in the same school for a long time and would benefit from a fresh perspective. Change can be reinvigorating, offer a fresh beginning, new outlook, and an opportunity to change old behavior patterns

Career Change

Some teachers behave badly because they are not happy teaching. They are in the wrong career. They became teachers because someone else wanted, encouraged, or expected them to do so. They spent four of five years of their life and a sizeable amount of money obtaining a teaching degree. Now they feel obligated to remain in a job that is unsatisfying to them. Disappointed and unhappy, they inflict misery on everyone around them. They may be reluctant to leave for several reasons: (a) abandoning teaching would disappoint someone, usually parents; (b) they don't know how to do anything else; and (c) the prospect of leaving makes them feel like they failed. Principals can offer a lifeline to these teachers by redirecting them into more satisfying careers. When a teacher seems unhappy in the profession, engage the individual in a friendly, casual conversation. "How is everything? You seem unhappy lately. Are you happy teaching?" If you hear a "no," ask what the teacher would rather be doing. Give assurances that it is okay to change professions. Assist the teacher in exploring other opportunities. One principal, who inherited several unhappy teachers, reported referring them to a career counselor. They found more satisfying careers and were grateful for the assistance. Helping unhappy teachers out of teaching and in to more suitable professions benefits everyone.

Termination—Nonrenewal

If a teacher's behavior in any way threatens the well-being of students, immediate action is required, including possible removal of the teacher from the classroom. Principals in our studies reported terminating teachers whose inappropriate behavior threatened the well-being of students, citing examples such as those that follow:

[The teacher] was using bad language on the coaching field.

A male teacher wanted to be "friends" with and "counsel" female [high school] students.

If termination or contract nonrenewal is on the horizon, appropriate documentation should be maintained, legal counsel sought, and strict adherence given to district policies and procedures.

Leave the Situation

Almost all of the principals we spoke with chose not to leave schools because of difficult teachers. They reported being capable of handling the situation. However, some principals reported being relieved when they were transferred or were able to retire.

Principals who find themselves in school settings that jeopardize their psychological well-being or physical safety would be wise to seek employment elsewhere. One of the principals in our study reported leaving a school not because of difficult teachers but because of an abusive supervisor.

TAKE ACTION!

- Examine district policies and procedures related to teacher behavior so that you know the rules and guidelines.
- Use your knowledge of the difficult teacher behaviors you identified at the conclusion of Chapters 1 and 2 to establish target behavioral changes for the teachers.
- Schedule a purposeful conversation with each teacher you have identified.

CHAPTER FOUR

Am I Contributing to the Problem?

Oh wad some power the giftie gie us, to see oursels as others see us.

—Robert Burns

- o Identifying your behavior
- o Anticipating problems
- o Monitoring your behavior

Principals, by virtue of their position, have enormous power over the work environment of a school and the treatment of the people who work there. Their attitude, demeanor, and behavior establish the tone of the school. Principals can create environments in which teachers look forward to Monday mornings or environments that contribute to teacher dissatisfaction and attrition. Principals can promote a spirit of cohesion and teamwork in the school.

When teachers perceive they are mistreated, the school climate becomes charged with resentment, hostility, mistrust, and withdrawal. Teachers feel compelled to hide mistakes and play it safe, rather than embrace innovation (Bassman, 1992). The related effects deter school progress and ultimately diminish student learning. Students suffer when teachers are unhappy. By contrast, when principals are caring and respectful toward teachers and treat them in a professional manner, teachers are more respectful toward students and more engaged in their teaching.

The Blind Spot in Behavior

Principals do not decide to become "difficult" people or "bully bosses." Most principals who are considered difficult are unaware of how others perceive them or how their behavior fosters difficult behavior in others. As observed by Luft and Ingham, the creators of the Johari Window (1955), all of us have a blind spot that others see, but we do not.

Difficult principals display a variety of behaviors that bring out the worst in teachers, while believing that they are good administrators who treat teachers fairly. In the words of one principal, "I've often wondered if one of my [difficult] teachers might not choose to leave at some point because [she] . . . doesn't feel that I am being supportive. I hope I am not choosing to be less than supportive in hopes that the person will leave. I try to find out what's good in people, so I hope I am supportive in other ways."

What does a difficult principal look like? Everyone is difficult sometimes; however, difficult principals display behavior that is considered difficult to a wide range of teachers over an extended time period. Blase and Blase (2003) are among a small number of researchers who have studied principal mistreatment of teachers. They identified principals' mistreatment behaviors as occurring at different levels of severity. The lowest form was indirect mistreatment, including discounting teachers' thoughts, needs, and feelings; isolating and abandoning teachers; withholding resources and opportunities; and showing favoritism. Although some of these principals may be unaware of their behavior or its effects, their mistreatment takes a personal toll on teachers' personal and professional lives.

Increasing in severity are principals who engage in direct acts of mistreatment that cannot be understood as a "blind spot" in their behavior. These principals engage in intolerable acts of deliberate and direct mistreatment of teachers and sometimes students. Blase and Blase (2003) describe these abusive principals as "authoritarian, coercive, and mean-spirited" individuals who "use formal and informal power against teachers." They perform direct and escalating acts of aggression, including "spying, sabotaging, stealing, and destroying teacher instructional aids, making unreasonable work demands, and both public and private criticism" (p. 140). Principals in the worst category include those who use "lying, being explosive and nasty, threats, unwarranted reprimands, unfair evaluations, mistreating students, sexual harassment, and racism" (Blase & Blase, 2003, p. 140). Principals who display these deliberately malicious actions are beyond the province of this book, as it is doubtful they are anxious to improve their behavior. This chapter is for principals who seek to uncover and improve behaviors that can derail their leadership and career path, and who want to treat teachers with the respect and fairness they deserve.

WHY ARE SOME PRINCIPALS "DIFFICULT"?

Causes of Difficult Behavior in Principals

- Inexperience
- Authoritarian Style
- Desire to Be Liked
- Seduced by Power

Difficult principals display a variety of behaviors, but each seeks the same goal, total control. They may verbally espouse teamwork, shared goals, teacher leadership, and consensus building, but in practice, they are authoritarian and controlling. Teachers complain that difficult principals do not communicate, are untrustworthy, show favoritism, do not share decision making, do not delegate, micromanage, do not support teachers, are not visible in the school, have a closed-door policy, do not interact with teachers, and do not maintain emotional control. Why does a principal who wants to be a team leader resort to controlling behavior?

Inexperience

A change of schools or a first-time principalship can trigger difficult behavior in some individuals. As we mentioned earlier, stressful situations are often the catalyst for the emergence of difficult behaviors. When individuals move to a new leadership position, unwanted behaviors can be triggered by the discomfort of the new role. Inexperience, insecurity, lack of skills, and the need to establish control may precipitate difficult behaviors. One principal reflecting on her first year said, "I do think I . . . lost a teacher because of my behavior that first year. I've often wondered about that. . . . I wasn't as good as I am now about pointing out deficiencies. I am much better at that now. . . it doesn't seem like I'm so accusatory. . . . I can be more objective about it, and I handle it better." Principals in their first year often report being more authoritarian than they thought they would be. Another principal said, "I felt so pressured by the enormity of tasks and the desire to do well. I didn't have time to collaborate; I just needed to get things done, so I resorted to telling people what to do." Other new principals try so hard to be collaborative that they appear indecisive. Frustrated teachers become weary of committees that meet endlessly with few substantive decisions to show for their efforts. For new principals, it takes time to acquire a balance between the need for collaboration and the need for principals to take action in decision making.

Authoritarian Style

Some veteran principals continue to use an authoritarian style of leadership. Although they know the benefits of and may want to be collaborative, they struggle to behave in a collaborative manner. When they feel pressured to perform, make a decision, or meet a deadline, their primary goal is to get the job done (Glickman et al., 2009). Thoughts of collaboration evaporate as they make unilateral decisions without involvement of stakeholders. Teachers soon learn that their opinions are not valued, and their needs are not considered important.

Desire to Be Liked

By contrast, some principals are difficult because they try to please everyone. They try to be all things to all people, form committees for every minute decision, make many promises, but do not follow through. They frustrate teachers who perceive them as indecisive, untrustworthy, and ineffective.

Addicted to Power

Power can be seductive and addictive. "Power tends to corrupt and absolute power corrupts absolutely" (Lord Acton, April 5, 1887). New principals can become enamored by their position and the power it affords them. One principal recalled using a new leadership role to retaliate against a former colleague. "When we were colleagues, she engaged in sabotage against me. When I became the school's administrator, I am ashamed to admit, I got my revenge by giving her unfavorable schedules and disagreeable assignments."

Veteran principals can become so comfortable with their power that they assume the role of monarchs overseeing not-so-loyal subjects. Teachers are treated like forced labor with little regard for them as individuals. Teachers tell tales of principals who seldom leave their office, do not speak to them in the hall, seldom visit their classrooms, and know few students' names. One teacher said, "We seldom see our principal, so we have a little joke using the title of a children's computer game: 'Where in the World Is Mrs. San Diego?'"

Teachers' Reactions

How do teachers react to a difficult principal? When teachers work with a difficult principal, some of them adopt a self-protection mode. They stay in their classrooms, try not to make waves, and cease to be innovative (Blase & Blase, 2003). Other teachers become angry and divisive, responding with difficult behaviors or forming toxic subcultures in retaliation. A few teachers leave the school or the profession. One teacher reported that her disenchantment motivated her to become a principal.

> I worked for a principal who was a [saboteur]. I was only a third-year teacher and never knew a boss could be this way. When I finally figured out what she was doing (it took me five more years), I was stunned. I enrolled in graduate school and two years later I had her job. I have this person to thank for giving me an example of what a principal is not.

COULD YOUR BEHAVIOR BE CONSIDERED DIFFICULT?

He who controls others may be powerful, but he who has mastered himself is mightier still.

—Lao Tzu

How can I tell if I am difficult? Most people are not aware that they are being difficult. Behavior patterns that others perceive as difficult are ingrained and habitual. Consequently, principals can be regarded as difficult by staff members and be totally unaware of their behavior.

Difficult Behaviors

Knowing what behaviors are considered difficult is useful when conducting a self-appraisal or designing a principal evaluation to be used by teachers. Difficult principals often engage in one or more of the following behaviors:

- Rigidity in Management
- Lack of Delegation
- Lack of Communication
- Lack of Recognition
- Not Listening to Teachers' Needs and Problems
- Defensive When Challenged
- Lack of Follow-Through
- Showing Favoritism
- Lack of Emotional Stability
- Lack of Visibility

Rigidity in Management

Are you perceived as domineering (your way or the highway) by the teachers? If so, you might hear yourself making statements such as, "That's just the way it is. There is no need for discussion because it isn't optional." Teachers tend to avoid and resist domineering principals. One principal told us, "I have to be really careful and make sure [my decision] is not a case of my wanting my own way. I have to ask myself if another way is acceptable."

Lack of Delegation

Do you do everything yourself? Some principals do everything themselves because they do not trust others to do things right. By doing so, they miss the opportunity to encourage teacher ownership and involvement in school initiatives. Additionally, potential teacher leaders are denied the opportunity to develop their talents and share their skills.

Lack of Communication

Do teachers complain about lack of information? Is gossip prevalent in your building? Two-way communication between the principal and staff is essential. Without it, conditions are ripe for distrust and confusion to develop. When people do not have the facts, they create their own. Rumors proliferate and the grapevine becomes the communication network.

Lack of Recognition

Do you thank teachers for their work and show appreciation for their efforts? Do you applaud their successes and recognize their achievements? Everyone needs to feel appreciated, valued for their work, and rewarded when they do well. Teachers who do not feel appreciated and valued become negative and cynical. Some suffer burnout.

Not Listening to Teachers' Needs and Problems

Do you provide an avenue for teachers to make suggestions, voice complaints, question decisions? Do you listen with full attention and an open mind when teachers talk to you? Two-way conversations and the use of good listening skills and open communication channels are essential. As one principal pointed out, "If a teacher takes the time to visit with me, I know that he or she considers the issue important. I need to listen attentively. I consider the time I spend listening as an investment in my relationship with that teacher and an opportunity to provide assistance." There is no need for a speedy response. The option is always available to tell the speaker that you need time to consider the suggestion or to find an answer to the question. Let the person know when you expect to have a response.

Defensive

How do you react when teachers complain or criticize you? Do you become angry or defensive, or do you try to understand their position? Conflicting ideas and positions should not be considered as negatives. Handled properly, conflict can generate new possibilities and better solutions.

Lack of Follow-Through

Is your leadership strewn with programs that were initiated but never fully implemented, broken promises, and important paperwork lost under stacks of clutter? Principals who do not follow through with initiatives or lose important documents cannot be trusted to fulfill promises and lose credibility with teachers.

Showing Favoritism

Do you show favoritism to one or two teachers? Although it is human nature to like some people more than others, displaying signs of personal preferences is unprofessional and destructive to staff morale. Teachers, like students, are quick to notice who receives attention and special treatment. The end result of favoritism is competition, divisiveness, and hurt feelings among the staff.

Lack of Emotional Stability

Do people tiptoe around you and check your daily mood before approaching you? Do your mood swings keep teachers and students on an emotional roller coaster—never knowing how you will respond? Do you lose your temper? Schools need leaders whose emotional health is stable and who can control their temper. Principals need to maintain their emotional and physical well-being, and they need to balance their work with time for rest, relaxation, and emotional outlets. Principals need to learn to leave their personal problems at home.

FERTILE GROUND FOR DIFFICULT TEACHERS

Principals in a new position who find themselves surrounded by difficult teachers might wonder, "Why is this happening?" Several factors may be involved.

A change of school leadership is stressful for teachers. Stress can trigger difficult behavior even from staff members who are normally cooperative. When a leadership change occurs, teachers who were previously cooperative may become resistant and difficult. Teachers who were chronically difficult may become even more difficult. Being aware of the potential for difficult behavior during times of stress can assist administrators in detecting, preventing, and dealing with unwanted behavior.

The past history of the school and circumstances surrounding the tenure of previous principals can all combine to create a challenging year for a new principal. The climate in a school may already be toxic when you arrive. Knowing the reasons for the difficult behaviors helps to depersonalize it and can be useful in determining a proper course of action. The following scenarios are worthy of consideration.

You Are a New Principal or New to the School

When a new principal is appointed, teachers are understandably anxious about how the new leader's personality will affect them and their teaching. Talking with teachers individually and listening to their concerns can be reassuring and diminish the emergence of negative behaviors.

Difficult teachers may see the change in leadership as an opportunity to lobby for their favorite cause and ask for favors. Anxious to gain favor with teachers, some new principals rush to please teachers and make promises they later regret. Delaying decisions until the teachers are known and situations have been carefully examined is a wiser choice. One principal remarked, "The first day in my office as the new principal, teachers with agendas came out of the woodwork telling me tales about my predecessor and asking for favors."

You Have Been Promoted From the Ranks

Beginning a principalship in a school and community you know makes some things easier. However, moving from the rank of teacher to principal in the same school brings another set of challenges in terms of establishing new relationships with former peers. Some former peers may be resentful or jealous of your new position and try to sabotage your success. One principal said, "When my appointment was announced, not one of my friends congratulated me. Instead, a few of them started malicious rumors about me." Since sabotage is a passive-aggressive behavior, it can be difficult to detect. The tools of saboteurs include malicious gossip, rumors, losing important material, forgetting deadlines, and other behaviors designed to make the principal appear incompetent. Awareness of the possibility of indirect aggression from former colleagues and friends is the first step in avoiding or curtailing it.

You Are Different in Some Way Than Previous Principals

Whenever a principal is different in any way from previous principals, difficult behaviors are more likely to emerge. Differences such as gender, race, ethnicity, and religion are among variations that create fertile ground for the emergence of difficult teachers. One African American principal observed, "The difficult teachers who happened to be African American became a problem when I refused to show them favoritism."

The Competitor for Your Position Works in the School

A principal whose competitor for the position remains employed in the school has a potential enemy. If the competitor is a difficult teacher, a problem is likely to emerge. If the teachers supported the competitor for the position, the problem multiplies. For principals, this is particularly challenging if the faculty members have formed close-knit friendships. The newly appointed principal may be a prime target of sabotage from the competitor and friends.

The School Has Had a Rapid Turnover of Principals

The rapid succession of principals can foster the emergence of negative teacher leaders who seize power and run the school. If the negative leaders have a strong following, the new principal will encounter a struggle to gain control and leadership of the school.

One principal reported, "My first week at school, I overheard one of the more difficult teachers telling a group of her colleagues, 'Just ignore her; she won't be here long. Just keep doing what we've been doing.'" Schools with rapid turnover in leadership are likely to have toxic subcultures.

Toxic School

When the school is dominated by toxic subcultures, the first task is to break up the toxic pods. Reorganize room assignments, teaching assignments, duties, schedules, seating at faculty meetings, whatever it takes to split up the toxic groups. Move people out of their comfort zones. Find the leaders and focus on their behaviors. Try to steer the followers into groups with positive leaders.

Your Predecessor Was Beloved

If your predecessor was well liked and had a long tenure at the school, the teachers may mourn that person's departure or retirement. Teachers who are deeply entrenched in the past, mourning a loss, or are enjoying the status quo may resent any changes you make. You may become an unwitting victim of the "Rebecca Myth" (Gouldner, 1954). "Named after du Maurier's novel *Rebecca*, the myth is about the process of idealizing predecessors regardless of their objective qualities" (Brock & Grady, 1995, p. 3). Regardless of the origin of their feelings for your predecessor, difficult teachers will be first to voice their disapproval and resist proposed changes. The new principal needs to do the following:

- Allow time for teachers to mourn;
- Avoid comments that appear critical of the predecessor;
- Develop personal relationships with staff members; and
- Make changes slowly.

Making small but favorable changes in the beginning can help build trust and support for the new leader when it is time for major changes.

Your Predecessor Died

You are following in the footsteps of a saint. Regardless of the person's favor among the faculty during their tenure, after death, the person assumes perfection. This is an emotional time for everyone in the school, including staff members, students, and parents. They need time to grieve, to reminisce about the person they lost, and to cherish the times they shared. It will grieve them to see someone else in the principal's office. Even small changes may seem objectionable to them.

Be careful not to criticize any actions of the predecessor. Do not take the teachers' behaviors toward you personally. Give everyone time and space to grieve. Listen to the teachers when they share stories about their lost leader; be respectful. In doing so, you will gain their trust and respect. Understand that the first year will be a challenge and memories last forever.

GENDER-RELATED DIFFERENCES IN DIFFICULT BEHAVIOR

Knowing the gender-related differences in difficult behavior is important for male and female principals. Researchers ascribe the differences in men and women's behavior to a variety of factors. Some researchers ascribe behavior differences to social construction, while others believe behavior is biologically determined. Researchers such as Gilligan, however, abhor the notion that behavior is either socially or biologically determined while ignoring the psychological determinants of humans (Gilligan, 1982). Regardless of one's stance in the debate, the fact remains—men and women do behave differently.

The differences in the early socialization of boys and girls are widely accepted. Societal norms are more accepting of overt aggression from boys than from girls. Physical confrontations and fighting are tolerated for boys, hence the adage, "Boys will be boys." Boys are encouraged to be assertive, use direct behaviors to solve their problems—to be leaders. By contrast, girls are taught to be gentle, cooperative, polite, and are admonished to "Be a good girl." Since overt aggression is not acceptable, girls have few opportunities to learn to be assertive. Thus, they use the less obvious passive-aggressive behaviors to get what they want. Since most of the leaders they know are male, they come to accept male dominance as part of life.

Researchers also ascribe male and female behaviors to differences in thought patterns between men and women. They purport that men are more competitive and concerned about maintaining hierarchies. Women are less competitive and more concerned with maintaining relationships (Gilligan, 1982). For example, during childhood, boys usually prefer games with a leader and rules. When a dispute arises, they resolve it and continue playing. By contrast, girls prefer games without rules and leaders. When a dispute occurs, they stop playing or change games to maintain relationships.

Regardless of the origin of the behavior, gender plays a role in men and women's choice of responses. When a man is displeased, he usually lets people know about it; however, women often keep people guessing. When a difficult man does not get his way, his responses might include the following: direct confrontation, verbal aggression, verbal bullying, overt anger, and in extreme situations (seldom in the workplace), physical aggression. A woman is more likely to use more covert, subtle, and indirect aggression such as sulking, holding grudges, ignoring, excluding, refusing to communicate, and malicious gossiping. Although there is a danger in oversimplification of gender differences, the fact that they exist and the expectation of these differences in behavior can create principal-to-teacher conflict and teacher-to-teacher conflict, particularly among women.

You Are a Woman Leader Among Women

When a woman is promoted to a leadership position in an educational setting, it is often her close women friends or colleagues who attempt to diminish perceptions of the new leader's credibility, capability, and sometimes morality. Their tools include malicious gossip, rumors, innuendoes, false reports to superiors, and withholding or losing information. The new principal, who is counting on the support of women friends and colleagues, is often confused and hurt by these behaviors. The effects of sabotage can be enduring, emotionally devastating, and professionally disastrous (Brock, 2008, April; Heim, Murphy, & Golant, 2001). A study by Culver (2007) reports the near burnout of a female principal who was the victim of indirect aggression by another woman.

The nature of women's relationships is fundamental to understanding woman-to-woman conflict. Relationships between women are important to women's sense of well-being. Women form close bonds of friendship and rely on each other for comfort, solace, advice, and companionship. Women's relationships are based on a flattened hierarchy in which friends have equal status. According to Chesler (2001), "Women demand an egalitarian, dyadic reciprocity and are, therefore, more threatened by the slightest change in status" (p. 109). Status is determined by a number of factors, including physical attributes, appearance, education, professional competence, and even family situation. When a woman becomes a principal, she changes status in the group thereby making some women feel inferior. The following circumstances are examples of situations primed for the emergence of conflict (Heim, Murphy, & Golant, 2001).

Newly Appointed Woman Principal

The appointment of a woman principal can create mixed responses from women faculty. Although some women will welcome the opportunity to work with a female leader, female faculty who aspire to leadership may be jealous and try to discredit her. Women who do not aspire to leadership may be resentful of the new woman principal because her achievement raises the bar of expectations for them and makes them feel inadequate.

Woman Principal Promoted From the Ranks

When a woman teacher is appointed principal of a school in which she taught, the mutual reciprocity of friendship assumes a new dynamic. As the newly appointed leader, she has the power to bestow or take away something desired by the other teachers (Heim, Murphy, & Golant, 2001). Previously supportive women friends, now threatened by the shift in power, may sabotage the friend who has advanced in her career. Their acts of sabotage can cause disruption to school goals and potential career damage and great emotional pain to the newly appointed principal (Brock, April 2008).

Expectation for Women's Leadership

Female teachers have different expectations for a woman principal than they do for a male principal. Men principals can use authoritative and hierarchical behaviors. Women leaders cannot. Women teachers expect a woman principal to be collaborative, egalitarian, and maintain a close relationship with teachers. If she is perceived otherwise, conflict will likely erupt. As Tanenbaum (2002) observed, "Women are caught in an impossible bind: We need to be competitive in order to be truly feminine, yet we can't be competitive because that would make us unwomanly" (p. 21). Prospective women leaders need to be aware of the dynamics of competition and indirect aggression to which some women subscribe. Acknowledging the existence of sabotage, discussing the dynamics, and examining the strategies that women can use to avoid it are important steps. The following strategies may reduce sabotage from other women:

- Be aware that not all women are worthy of your trust and willing to support you.
- Be discerning when selecting confidants, mentors, and collaborators.
- Separate personal and professional relationships.
- Be discrete in the information you share; leave personal information at home.
- Document your actions.
- Avoid or downplay displays of status symbols that trigger resentment.
- Act with self-confidence; saboteurs prefer people who appear vulnerable.
- Relate to other women in ways that elevate their self-esteem.
- Use and model assertive behaviors when dealing with conflict.
- Confront known saboteurs about their behavior; call them on their actions.
- Refuse to listen to or participate in gossiping, backstabbing, and other acts of sabotage; name it when you hear it or see it.
- Be proactive in mentoring and supporting other women. (Brock, 2008, April)

Dealing With Woman-to-Woman Sabotage

When acts of sabotage are detected, the first step is to determine the level of importance or effect of the act. If the act is minor, insignificant, or a onetime situation, the situation is best ignored. However, if acts of indirect aggression are destructive to the leader's credibility, reputation, ability to lead, or interfere with the school's goals, principals need to take action (Brock & Grady, 2006).

- Meet with the teacher in private.
- Calmly explain what you have learned.
- Correct misperceptions.
- Express your disappointment at the unacceptable behavior.
- Let the person know that the behavior will not be tolerated.
- End the meeting by expressing a desire to forget the past and look toward the future.
- If the sabotage continues, build a case for termination.
- Do not harbor the hurt or allow the experience to undermine your confidence. (Brock, 2008, July; Brock & Grady, 2006; Kosmoski & Pollack, 2000)

STRATEGIES FOR CHANGE

Shared Decision Making

Do you share decision making or simply appoint committees? Teachers who spend time on committees expect to be the decision makers or at least make a contribution to the final decision. When their input is not considered, teachers feel manipulated and devalued.

Personal Relationships

Do you know each teacher personally? Everyone likes to be known and valued as a person. Having a personal relationship with each teacher is essential. This can be accomplished by spending a few minutes each day talking with each teacher about matters other than school.

Praise and Recognition

Do you frequently offer sincere praise for specific accomplishments? Do you publicly recognize teachers for their work? Teaching can seem like a thankless job when the only positive feedback a teacher receives comes from a few parents and an occasional student. Principals play a critical role in noticing and praising teachers for their efforts and accomplishments. As one retired principal observed, "I worked with some extraordinary teachers, and my biggest regret is that I did not offer them enough praise and recognition.

Objective Feedback

Do you offer objective feedback or pass judgments? If you tell a teacher that, "Three parents have called today to complain that you kept your class in from recess yesterday, you are stating facts. The teacher will likely offer additional explanation, and you can discuss the wisdom of that decision with the teacher. By contrast, if you say, "Poor discipline is causing me all sorts of problems!" The teacher will react defensively to the judgmental statement, and the ensuing conversation may be unproductive.

Sense of Humor

Do you laugh at yourself when you make a mistake? Do you have fun with teachers? Laughter improves attitudes and outlooks;

makes school a welcoming place; and makes learning pleasurable for students. When teachers enjoy the company of the principal and each other, they enjoy coming to work and are more likely to include laughter in their classrooms.

Monitoring Tools

Principals need help to "see themselves as others see them." They can gain this information by seeking input about their behavior from subordinates and superiors. Principals tell teachers who experience classroom management problems to first consider their own behavior and how they might be contributing to it. In similar fashion, principals should ask themselves if their behavior is triggered or contributing to difficult teacher behavior. One reported doing just that, "When teachers complain, I re-examine my decisions and my behavior to see if there is any truth in their complaints."

Observe Teachers' Reactions

One way to determine if your behavior is considered difficult by your staff is to observe how teachers respond to you. Their responses offer clues about how they perceive you and how approachable you are to them. Your answers to the following questions can offer insights into how others perceive you:

- How would your teachers describe you to others?
- How do teachers react when you enter the faculty room?
- What do teachers do when you drop by their classroom?
- How do teachers respond when they see you in the hallway?
- How do teachers behave when you conduct faculty meetings?
- How do teachers react when you propose a change?
- Do teachers drop by your office to share funny incidents that occur in their classroom?
- Do teachers drop by your office to discuss concerns related to teaching or students?
- Do teachers tell you about their families or personal lives?
- Do teachers ever kid, tease, or pull humorous pranks on you?
- What is the annual rate of teacher turnover in the school?

Ask Teachers

A second way to obtain feedback on your behavior is to ask the teachers. Ask them to complete an annual review of your performance. Since teachers will be reluctant to offer negative feedback to a difficult principal, responses to performance reviews need to be anonymous. A tool for teachers to evaluate the principal can be found at the end of the chapter.

Ask Your Supervisor

A third way to obtain feedback on your behavior is to ask your supervisor to evaluate your performance at least once a year. Have a conversation about your strengths and weaknesses and about how others perceive you. Ask your supervisor for suggestions on improving your performance.

Listen to Needs

Routinely meet with individuals and small groups and ask teachers for input on how you can assist them. Initiate the conversation by saying, "My job is to help you. In order to do that, I need to be aware of your needs. What can I do to assist you?" This approach will become comfortable for teachers and will produce valuable information to guide your actions. Remember teachers will expect you to act on the information they share with you. Be prepared to follow through.

Once you have collected the information about your performance, determine which of your behaviors are not effective and make the necessary changes. Although the information may surprise and dismay you, teachers' perceptions are their reality. Knowing how your behavior is perceived is a prerequisite to making improvements and thereby creating a more cooperative and collaborative school community.

TAKE ACTION!

- Use the Teacher's Evaluation of the Principal's Performance to gather information about how others see you.
- Use the information from the evaluations to identify three to five personal improvements goals.

PART 1: TEACHER'S EVALUATION OF THE PRINCIPAL'S PERFORMANCE

Check the appropriate column using the following scale:

5 = Outstanding; 4 = Exceeds expectations; 3 = Satisfactory; 2 = Needs improvement; 1 = Unsatisfactory

Teacher's Evaluation of the Principal's Performance					
THE PRINCIPAL:	5	4	3	2	1
Values me as a person					
Respects me as a teacher					
Listens to my needs and problems					
Appreciates my efforts					
Treats me fairly					
Avoids favoritism					
Recognizes my achievements					
Encourages my professional growth					
Listens objectively to input from teachers					
Shares decision making					
Follows through on decisions					
Keeps promises					
Is trustworthy					
Demonstrates emotional stability					
Keeps personal problems out of school					
Distributes duties fairly					
Is visible in the building					

PART 2: TEACHER'S EVALUATION OF THE PRINCIPAL'S PERFORMANCE

Average the scores of the teachers' evaluations of the principal. Circle the average score for each item from Part 1. For items with an average of 2 (needs improvement) or 1 (unsatisfactory), determine the changes you want to make to improve your performance in that area.

Teacher's Evaluation of the Principal's Performance		
THE PRINCIPAL:	*Score*	*Changes I will make to improve performance:*
Values me as a person	5 4 3 2 1	
Respects me as a teacher	5 4 3 2 1	
Listens to my needs and problems	5 4 3 2 1	
Appreciates my efforts	5 4 3 2 1	
Treats me fairly	5 4 3 2 1	
Avoids favoritism	5 4 3 2 1	
Recognizes my achievements	5 4 3 2 1	
Encourages my professional growth	5 4 3 2 1	
Listens objectively to input from teachers	5 4 3 2 1	
Shares decision making	5 4 3 2 1	
Follows through on decisions	5 4 3 2 1	
Keeps promises	5 4 3 2 1	
Is trustworthy	5 4 3 2 1	
Demonstrates emotional stability	5 4 3 2 1	
Keeps personal problems out of school	5 4 3 2 1	
Distributes duties fairly	5 4 3 2 1	
Is visible in the building	5 4 3 2 1	

Part III

Prevention

CHAPTER FIVE

Interpersonal Skills That Help

Too often we underestimate the power of a touch, a smile, a kind word, a listening ear, an honest compliment, or the smallest act of caring, all of which have the potential to turn a life around.

—Leo F. Buscaglia

○ Listening to understand

○ Speaking for understanding

○ Using body language

○ Diffusing emotionally charged conversations

W hen consistent, positive communication exists between the principal and staff members, a foundation of trust necessary for a harmonious and collaborative community exists. By contrast, when consistent, positive communication is missing, the stage is set for difficult behavior to flourish.

Trusting relationships discourage difficult behaviors.

A principal's effectiveness as a leader depends on communication. Principals spend significant time each day communicating with teachers, office assistants, auxiliary staff, students, parents, district personnel, visitors, and vendors. The effectiveness of their communication determines the level of satisfaction and trust that is generated among community members.

Principals who routinely listen to concerns, discuss differences, and share information garner trust and respect while learning valuable information that equips them to lead more effectively. Principals who fail to listen will not be aware of existing problems or will not have the necessary information to solve them. They will lack the referent power required of influential leaders (French & Raven, 1959, pp. 150–167). Poor communication establishes a breeding ground for the emergence of difficult teachers and the formation of toxic subcultures.

Communication is a two-way process that requires mutual understanding of the message transmitted. Talking does not ensure that a message is understood and neither does listening. Message interference may emerge somewhere in the middle of a transmission and can occur from a variety of sources. If a speaker's message is inappropriate for the audience, lacks focus, clarity, or precise word choices, the listener may misinterpret the

Figure 5.1

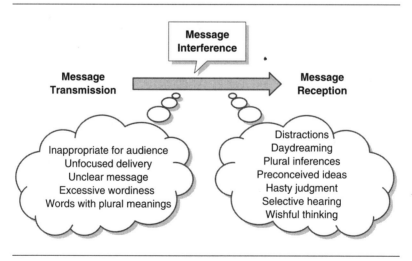

speaker's intended message. If listeners are distracted, daydreaming, misinterpret word meanings, have preconceived ideas, or make premature judgments, they may misinterpret a message. If any of these conditions exist, message transmission is clouded and communication does not occur.

LISTENING TO UNDERSTAND

To listen well, is as powerful a means of influence as to talk well, and is as essential to all true conversation.

—Chinese Proverb

Busy principals are interrupted many times each day by individuals who want to speak with them for "just a moment." When deadlines are tight and paperwork is mounting, it is tempting to listen halfheartedly while continuing to work. Doing so, however, conveys a message of disrespect to the speaker and invites misunderstandings. A better choice is to prepare yourself to listen and give the speaker full attention, thereby conveying respect and improving your chances of understanding the issue. One principal explained, "If people take the time to come to my office to speak with me, they have something to say that is obviously important to them. If it is important to them; I need to know about it. They deserve my full attention."

Listening is a skill that requires practice.

Although deceptively simple, listening is an acquired skill that requires practice. There is a vast difference between hearing and listening. Hearing occurs when we are aware of a person speaking. Listening occurs when we focus attentively, concentrate on what is being said, and try to understand the speaker's meaning.

Often we *think* we are listening when in reality, we are distracted by someone or something else or thinking about what we want to say. Part of the problem is the difference between the number of words we can speak and the number we can listen to per minute. People speak at a rate of 100 to 175 words per minute, but they can listen to up to 300 words per minute. This leaves substantial time for the listener to daydream or become distracted by other thoughts. Unless we listen with purpose, we may slip into reverie and miss the message intended by the speaker. Steps in active listening involve the following: making the speaker feel welcome, listening attentively, monitoring body language, and checking for understanding. Practicing the following steps can help:

- Welcome the Speaker
- Listen Silently
- Think About the Words
- Keep an Open Mind
- Reflect on the Message
- Evaluate the Information

Welcome the Speaker

Put away whatever you were doing. Stand and welcome the visitor with a smile. Move to a place where you can sit next to each other. Invite the person to speak by using "door-openers" (Bolton, 1979, p. 40). These may include describing the persons' body language and inviting them to share whatever is on their mind. The conversation might sound like, "Come in, Mrs. Peterson. I'm glad to see you. What's on your mind today?" If the person's body language reveals strong emotion, begin by acknowledging the emotion, "You look like you are upset. What seems to be wrong?" Then listen without interruption.

Listen Silently

Remain silent while others are speaking. Clearly, this is easier said than done. The natural tendency is to fill in gaps in conversations and to add opinions when others speak. Doing so, however, interrupts the speaker and may inhibit the flow of information.

The ability to listen silently while others speak is a powerful tool. Silence conveys respect and interest. It gives the speaker time to think and elaborate on the message; it nudges the reluctant speaker into sharing more extensively. Principals who practice attentive silence will discover that people often solve their own problems by the time they finish sharing them. Similarly, conflicts are often resolved by giving people an opportunity to "be heard."

Think About the Words

Listening to understand requires active participation. Think about what the speaker is saying. Listen for underlying emotions as well as words. Identify key points. Use encouraging nods of the head, changing facial expressions, and quiet "uh-huhs" and "I sees" to encourage, but do not interrupt. Change positions if you find your mind wandering. Ask yourself mental questions to remain focused.

Keep an Open Mind

Do not jump to conclusions or pass judgment until you have heard the entire message. Try to understand the situation from the speaker's perspective. How would you feel if this was your problem? What would you want done?

Reflect on the Message

When the speaker is finished speaking, reflect the message you heard by summarizing it in your own words. Ask the person if your understanding is correct. If it is not accurate, ask questions until you understand the message. Clarify what action the speaker wants you to take.

Evaluate the Information

Consider the facts presented. Evaluate their validity, reliability, and merit in light of what you know. What are the facts? Do you need additional information?

The Value of Listening

Most of the successful people I've known are the ones who do more listening than talking.

—Bernard M. Baruch

Listening is the key to knowing what teachers need, what motivates them, and how they feel about issues. These are the building blocks to establishing teamwork and collaboration in a school. When school leaders actively listen, they develop trusting relationships with staff members who

- Feel respected.
- Feel their ideas are worthwhile.
- Are encouraged to contribute their ideas.
- Feel safe to express their concerns.
- Often solve their own problems during the process of sharing them.
- Are less likely to engage in negative and disruptive behavior.

Engaging in purposeful or active listening keeps the focus on the speaker's message. Use the Evaluation of Listening Skills at the end of the chapter and on page 147 in the Resources section as a self-assessment.

Steps in Active Listening

A summary of steps in active listening include the following:

- Stop what you are doing.
- Stand up and welcome the speaker with a smile.
- Clear away distractions; move from behind your desk and sit near the speaker.
- Look at the speaker.
- Focus on the message being delivered; repeat the message in your mind.
- Listen without interrupting.
- Give nonverbal signals (i.e., nodding or changing facial expressions to indicate that you are listening).
- Be aware of underlying emotions in the speaker's message.
- Ask questions to clarify understanding.
- Avoid making a judgment until the speaker has finished.
- Restate the message you heard and check for accuracy.
- Evaluate the information.

SPEAKING FOR UNDERSTANDING

Think before you speak. If possible, postpone speaking until you have had a chance to think about the message you want to convey and how to convey it. Before speaking, reflect on the following:

- The listeners
- The purpose of the message
- The main point you want to convey
- Your choice of words
- Your tone of voice
- Your nonverbal behavior

Listener Considerations

Who is the intended audience? The content and delivery of a message for staff members needs to be different than the content and delivery of a message for parents, students, or community. Before preparing or delivering a message, consider the interests of the intended audience. How much information does your audience want or need? If students and parents will be in attendance, consider the educational level and language of the audience.

The Purpose of the Communication

The purpose of the communication sets the tone for the entire message. Word choice, delivery style, and the speaker's demeanor vary according to the level of formality needed for the occasion. Delivering an unpleasant or sad message requires more formality than welcoming staff members to a holiday gathering.

Make the Point

> *Make sure you have finished speaking before your audience has finished listening.*
>
> —Dorothy Sarnoff

Most of us at some point have been frustrated victims of speakers who talked *around* their topic, never clearly and succinctly conveying the main point of their message. Oblivious to the audience's impatience, they continue to talk.

Keep the message focused and brief. Begin with the most important fact you want to convey. Continue with supporting statements. End with a brief concluding comment or summary of the message. Share only the information that the audience needs or wants to know. Choose words that express your meaning. Avoid education lingo, acronyms, and extraneous words.

If you have time, write your message before delivering it. When you read your message, everything you say should reflect back to your opening statement; if it does not, eliminate it. Delivering a message that is clear and concise seems simple; however, it requires practice. Remember the following sequence when developing your message:

- First: The most important fact or idea
- Second: Statements to support the most important fact or idea
- Third: The least important or minor details
- Fourth: Concluding or summary statement

To use the words of Winston Churchill, "Say what you have to say, and when you come to a sentence with a grammatical ending, sit down."

Choose Words Carefully

Some words and phrases convey more than one meaning, are easily misinterpreted, or are emotionally loaded. Consider the various meanings that can be construed by the following sentences, "Implementing the new reading program was quite an experience." "My new office assistant is really something." We can ascribe a variety of meanings—positive and negative—to each sentence. Using more precise language eliminates possible misinterpretations of the intended meaning. Relying on voice intonations and body language to clarify messages may be helpful; however, when messages are taken out of context and retold in the faculty lounge or on the soccer field, imprecise language is more easily misconstrued and misinterpreted.

Emotionally charged words can be effective and influential when used appropriately. However, the effective use of emotionally charged words requires knowledge of the audience and their current thoughts on the topic. Words that generate high emotion toward a positive goal for one group may incite hostility and anger in another group.

Cultural and religious beliefs and politically correct language are additional considerations. Words and casual phrases that are routinely used and considered appropriate and positive with one group or individual may not be in another group. As an example, one principal reported casually wishing someone, "Good luck!" and being shocked when the person was offended. To some people, the word "luck" refers to good fortune, for others, fate or karma. For this person, "luck" was equated with superstition and therefore in conflict with his belief that good fortune flows from Divine Providence. Being aware of the culture and religious beliefs of the audience and sensitive to language regarded as politically correct can minimize offending someone.

The Tone

Your tone of voice affects the listeners' interpretation of your message. For example, consider how a lack of enthusiasm, sincerity, or the barest hint of sarcasm in your tone can change the interpretation of the words, "Nice job" from a positive to a negative.

Most of us are conscious of our tone of voice when speaking before a large audience. However, when responding to daily interruptions and mountainous telephone messages and e-mails, it is easy for negative tones to slip by our radar. One principal reported being horrified when she listened to a message she had left someone and heard the negativity and impatience in her voice. Another principal reported dismay and embarrassment when someone commented on the negative tone of an e-mail she sent in haste.

As a solution, one author suggested smiling before you answer the phone (Condrill & Bough, 2007) or send an e-mail. Although people cannot see the smile, they will hear it in the tone of your voice and in your words. This tip also works when greeting visitors. When Miss Constance Complainer needs *one minute* of your time, put a smile on your face and think of some of her positive traits. Your tone of voice will be more positive and the end result of the meeting more satisfactory. Use the Evaluation of Speaking Skills at the end of the chapter and on page 148 in the Resources section as a self-assessment.

BODY LANGUAGE

While listening and speaking, monitor the nonverbal message that you are conveying. Guard against unwittingly revealing your feelings through your body language. Be aware of your facial expressions, your composure, and your posture. Although unspoken, these messages speak more loudly than words. Before a challenging conversation, take a deep breath, temporarily table other concerns, and put a smile on your face. Act as if this is the most important event of the day—because it is for the person who is speaking to you.

Standing, smiling, shaking hands, and sitting next to someone indicate openness to a speaker. Making eye contact, giving nonverbal and verbal encouragement, and maintaining full attention to the person who is speaking indicate interest in the speaker. By contrast, remaining behind your desk or crossing your arms or legs can indicate defensiveness, hostility, or lack of interest. Avoiding eye contact, staring expressionlessly at the speaker, looking at someone or something else, or interrupting the speaker to answer the phone sends a message that you have far more important things to do.

Use pacing to put a speaker at ease. Pacing is a technique used to establish rapport and let a speaker know you take the conversation seriously. It involves subtly adjusting your posture and the rate and intonation of your speech to match that of the speaker. Doing so demonstrates acceptance and respect for the speaker and aids in establishing rapport. Notice how you do this automatically when talking with a longtime friend. Although our behavior is more formal during professional meetings, the use of subtle pacing can increase the comfort level of visitors.

Watch the Speaker's Nonverbal Language

Pay attention to the body language that may reveal the speaker's underlying emotions. The speaker's nonverbal language provides clues about feelings that might not be expressed in words. Intense emotion, such as anxiety, grief, and anger are usually easy to detect. However, disappointment, disagreement, displeasure, sadness, and hurt feelings are easier to conceal and may be more difficult to detect. Recognizing their presence, however, is critical to understanding the speaker's message (Pawlas & Oliva, 2008).

If emotion is suspected but not expressed, silence can be used to encourage additional conversation. When the person appears to have finished speaking, remain silent for a while. The speaker will feel compelled to fill the silence by expanding on the message and becoming more forthcoming.

Nonverbal Cues

Signals of Approval	Signals of Disapproval
Smiles	Smirks or frowns
Nods	No head movement
Facing you	Turning aside
Making eye contact	Eye avoidance; glare; hostile stare
Relaxed arms	Arms folded across chest
Hands folded/resting on desk	Hands flat on desk; clenched fists
Fingers relaxed	Fingers pointed in pyramid; tapping
Legs crossed toward you	Legs crossed away from you; swinging
Feet quiet	Feet tapping
Leaning forward	Leaning backward; hands clasped behind neck
Body appears relaxed	Body appears tense/stiff

DIFFUSING EMOTIONALLY CHARGED CONVERSATIONS

Principals are required to make difficult decisions. In the process, they cannot please everyone. Sooner or later, someone will become angry and a confrontation will occur. When a principal confronts a difficult teacher, there may be an angry response. There is no way to make these situations pleasant. However, knowing how to approach and speak with an angry individual can prepare the way to a more successful outcome.

Difficult teachers want their own way. We should assume they will not be pleased when confronted about their inappropriate behavior. They will probably become upset, possibly enraged. You will become the enemy—the obstacle in their path. Following are tips for conversations with difficult teachers who are upset or angry.

**Tips for Dealing With
Emotionally Charged Conversations**

- If you or the teacher is angry or upset, wait until the emotion subsides before initiating a discussion about the problem.
- Speak with the person privately.
- Remain emotionally detached.
- Separate the person from the problem.
- Listen intently, respond calmly, and make sure your body language matches your words.
- Be respectful; imagine yourself in the person's situation.
- End the conversation if a teacher is verbally abusive.

Difficult teachers want and are accustomed to getting their own way. When you interfere, they may become emotional. Some of them will act hurt, possibly cry, and become angry or defensive. Their goal is to make you feel like a heartless bully and derail the conversation. They will offer excuses and try to convince you that the situation is beyond their control; they are blameless victims. Others will become angry and blame you for the problem. Difficult teachers do not want to accept responsibility for their behavior.

Do not engage in arguments with them, accept blame for their problems, or be swayed by their emotional fervor. Some principals prepare for conversations with difficult teachers by keeping a written statement of the problem behavior and the expected change in front of them. When the teacher tries to steer the conversation in a different direction, the principal keeps the conversation on track by repeating what is written on the prepared statement. "That may be so, but the situation we are discussing is _____ and I need you to _____ ." Lee and Marlene Canter's (1976) "broken record" technique is equally useful with difficult teachers as it is with difficult students. Use the same words, tone, volume, and intonation every time you repeat your request.

If either you or the teacher is angry or upset, wait until the emotion subsides before initiating a discussion about the problem. Confronting or engaging in conversation with a teacher when emotions are out of control is pointless and may even exacerbate the situation. You might suggest, "I can see that you are upset by this" or "I cannot discuss this right now." "Let's take some time to reflect or 'sleep on it' [the situation]. How about meeting tomorrow to discuss it?"

Have the conversation in a private place. This is a personnel issue and by definition should be confidential. Engaging in a debate in view of others is not only unprofessional but will also contribute to additional discord and division among the faculty.

Remain emotionally detached. Do not take inappropriate behaviors personally, allow a difficult teacher to snare you into their emotional web, or engage you in a debate. View the problem as belonging to the teacher. When someone is persistently critical, negative, or interferes with our leadership, it is difficult not to take it personally. Some principals reported feeling hurt or angry by difficult teachers' behaviors. One principal told us, "When I see that teacher, I want to go the other way . . . to avoid coming in contact with her." Regardless of how you feel, it is important to present an external demeanor that is calm, composed, and in control.

Separate the person from the problem. Consider your attitude toward the person. If we assign a label to a person, "Mary is such a complainer," then we tend to treat that person as a bother. We may not offer the person our full attention or take the person's issues seriously. Even if we pretend to listen, our body language says otherwise. If a teacher takes the time to speak with you, that person clearly considers the issue a problem and deserves your unbiased attention. First, give the teacher your full attention. Second, consider the possibility that although this person is a chronic complainer, a real problem may exist. Although this person has needlessly "called wolf" in the past, perhaps this time there really is a wolf! And finally, if the behavior is annoying to you yet does not interfere with any aspect of school life, perhaps a better choice is having a private chuckle rather than a confrontation. One principal shared a story about a teacher who hated change. During meetings when change was announced, the teacher listened without comment. The next morning like clockwork, she would appear in the office with a litany of reasons why the change would never work. After stating her opinion, however, she always cooperated without complaint. She merely wanted to "voice her opinion." The principal expected and accepted this behavior from the teacher and anticipated a visit each time a change was announced.

Listen intently, respond calmly, and make sure your body language matches your words. Assume the stance of an interested fact finder. Do not agree with the person or make promises. Remember, unless someone is in grave peril or the building is on fire, you do not have to respond immediately. Allow yourself time to think about the issue. Employ an appropriate phrase such as "Thank you for sharing" or "I will look into that."

Be respectful to the teacher and insist on respect toward yourself. However, if a teacher is verbally abusive, end the conversation. Tell the teacher, "I will meet with you when you have regained emotional control" and abandon the meeting. Later, schedule an appointment to meet with the teacher. Let the individual know that verbal abuse will not be tolerated.

Do not expect immediate improvement. In fact, the behavior may become worse for a while. Difficult people have been difficult for a long time. Many of them have practiced these behaviors since childhood. This is what works for them; they will not be eager to change. You will need to continue whatever behavior-change strategy you select until they are no longer *comfortable* with the old behavior. In some cases, the behavior is so entrenched that the difficult teacher may transfer to another school rather than adopt a new behavior.

Danger Alert

Occasionally, an individual will respond to constructive criticism, a performance review, or potential loss of employment with threats or implied threats of violence to self or others. When dealing with an agitated individual, Bell and Smith (2002) suggest watching for red alerts that include the following: references to self-violence, threats to you or others, threats against the school, and nonverbal expressions, such as kicking, throwing, or pounding on something. These red flags should be taken very seriously. Media accounts of upset employees returning to harm others and themselves in the workplace have become familiar occurrences.

If a person hints at self-violence, the administrators should take the person seriously, record the exact words and circumstances, and offer reassurance. Public safety, human resources, and district officials should be advised of the situation, and counseling resources sought for immediate intervention. The person should return home until the situation is resolved (Bell & Smith, 2002).

Threats and implied threats against persons or property and nonverbal hostility should be recorded and reported to individuals who have been named in the threat, superiors, human resources, and public safety personnel for follow up. If the situation is imminently dangerous, law enforcement should be called (Bell & Smith, 2002).

TAKE ACTION!

- Use the Evaluation of Listening Skills and the Evaluation of Speaking Skills to gather information about your strengths and weaknesses.
- Keep the Steps in Active Listening posted where you can review them daily.
- Post the Nonverbal Cues where they can be reviewed before or after conversations.

EVALUATION OF LISTENING SKILLS

Use the following rating sheet to conduct a self-evaluation; then ask teachers to evaluate you.

Check the appropriate rating for each statement:

5 = Outstanding; 4 = Exceeds expectations; 3 = Satisfactory; 2 = Needs improvement; 1 = Unsatisfactory

Teacher's Evaluation of the Principal: Listening Skills					
THE PRINCIPAL:	5	4	3	2	1
Is a good listener.					
Seems pleased when I ask to speak with him or her.					
Stops working; gives me full attention when I am speaking.					
Is interested in what I am saying.					
Listens without interrupting me.					
Asks questions to clarify my message.					
Repeats my message to check for understanding.					

EVALUATION OF SPEAKING SKILLS

Use the following rating sheet to conduct a self-evaluation; then ask teachers to evaluate you.

Check the appropriate rating for each statement:

5 = Outstanding; 4 = Exceeds expectations; 3 = Satisfactory; 2 = Needs improvement; 1 = Unsatisfactory

Teacher's Evaluation of the Principal: Speaking Skills					
THE PRINCIPAL:	5	4	3	2	1
Is an engaging and interesting speaker.					
Responds to questions with clear and concise answers.					
Gets to the point when sharing information.					
Uses language that is easily understood.					
Answers questions or e-mails in a respectful tone of voice.					
Checks for understanding and offers necessary clarification.					

CHAPTER SIX

Creating a Culture of Teamwork

○ Building a positive culture

○ Focusing on positive teachers

○ Creating a spirit of teamwork

○ Rewarding positive people

People want to feel that who they are and what they do matter. We now spend over 60% of our life at work and want that work to be connected with what we believe is important in the world. People want to be able to come to a place of work where they feel loved, appreciated, and cared about rather than demeaned, ignored, or taken for granted. And finally, everyone wants to hear the words, "Thank you. You make a difference."

—Jack Canfield, *The Heart at Work*

Preventing problems is easier and preferable to fixing problems. The principals in our studies focused on how they created positive school cultures to minimize the possibility of difficult behavior. They made people a priority. They developed relationships with individuals and took action to ensure that teachers felt appreciated and satisfied with their work experiences. In doing so, they weakened the power of negative teachers and returned the power to the positive teachers. They created school cultures in which teamwork was a valued norm.

Teamwork requires individuals who share a mind-set of cooperation and a willingness to work in a selfless manner toward school goals. Teamwork requires honesty, trust, flexibility, tolerance, and communication. Team members are willing to do the following:

- Share ideas, information, and resources
- Compromise
- Comply with group decisions
- Share the rewards of success

Teachers who feel valued and appreciated are more likely to contribute to team efforts and less likely to engage in difficult behaviors. A school's most valuable resource is its teachers. Their combined actions and interactions determine the level of student learning, the culture and climate of the school, the satisfaction of the school's public, and ultimately, whether or not a school meets its goals. Wise school leaders are aware of the importance of teachers and take steps to ensure high levels of teacher satisfaction. They know and value each teacher as a person, and they are attuned to the problems that teachers experience. As Beaudoin and Taylor (2004) observed, "No school culture can be truly addressed in any significant way until the context and the experiences of people are well understood" (p. 3).

BUILDING A POSITIVE CULTURE

A school's culture influences everything that happens and affects every person. Peterson (1999) described culture as "the beliefs, attitudes, and behaviors which characterize a school" (p. 1). Teachers are talking about culture when they say, "It's the way we do things here." In schools with positive cultures, common goals permeate the school. There is order and discipline, agreement on curriculum and instructional strategies, honest communication, and an abundance of humor and trust. Teachers feel supported by the school's administration.

First and foremost, it is all about creating a school culture that is rich in relationships. As Wagner (2004) observed, "Schools are feeling places, rich in relationships, nurturing, and caring . . . or at least they should be" (p. 11). In the quest for school reform, curriculum alignment, and assessment strategies, have we forgotten about the people? Have we overlooked the importance of relationships? Have we allowed negativity to seep under the school door? If the teachers and students are dissatisfied and the culture of the school is unhealthy, curriculum reform efforts and new assessment strategies will not be effective.

If a school's culture is unhealthy, a quick fix is not the answer. Although the outward appearances of a school can be quickly altered, changing the personality of a school takes time. Achieving and maintaining a healthy school culture is an ongoing process, one that requires monitoring, evaluation, and routine readjustment (Joyce & Showers, 2002). As needs change, the culture must adjust; old norms must be abandoned, replaced, or reshaped. Topchik (2001) suggests a four-step process for changing norms: (1) Conduct a cultural audit by describing the culture you have, (2) Describe what you want the new culture to be; specify what new norms will replace old norms, (3) Develop an action plan for each norm change, and (4) Implement the action plans; follow up to make sure new norms are developing; reward those who change; hold those accountable who do not.

Break Up Toxic Pods

Collegial and professional learning communities are prerequisites for effective schools (Glickman, Gordon, & Ross-Gordon, 2007; Sergiovanni & Starratt, 2002). When the negative or disruptive behaviors of teachers threaten the learning community, effective leaders must re-establish a more desirable balance.

When cultures are ignored and become outmoded, destructive behaviors can become the norm. The school culture can develop dysfunctional values, beliefs, and ways of interacting. Deal and Peterson (1998) refer to these as toxic cultures. In toxic school cultures, difficult teachers can be found in large numbers. As long as subcultures of toxic teachers are allowed to exist, there is little hope of developing a healthy school culture.

Group Effort

Everyone must become involved in improving the school's culture. This is not a task that a principal can mandate. Begin by talking with teachers about the impact of the school's culture on them, their teaching, and on student learning. Identify the needed improvements and take steps to accomplish your goals.

Lessen the influence of the negative teachers so positive teachers can assert leadership and make desired changes. As one principal suggested, "Break up toxic pods of teachers. Transfer them out. Separate them. . . ."

Defusing Negative Power

Toxic teachers band together in clusters or pods. They derive their power from each other. Breaking up the group and moving them out of proximity to each other helps to defuse their influence. Patterns and habits formed over time will not disappear overnight. In fact the behavior of toxic teachers may worsen when you remove them from the security of their group. Do it anyway. Mingling with a group of positive teachers may eventually motivate positive behavior change for negative teachers. Additionally, separating the negative teachers will make meetings more productive and lunch and planning periods more pleasant for the rest of the faculty. Consider the following suggestions:

- Re-assign classrooms; a new location and new neighbors work wonders.
- Re-assign grade levels; a change in curriculum can revitalize a teacher.
- Change planning times so toxic group members are not together.
- Change lunch times to break up the group.
- Hold several meetings with small groups of teachers instead of one large group.
- If necessary, transfer the ringleader of the toxic group to a different school; the intent is not to give someone else your problem but rather to use change to revitalize the teacher.
- If serious behaviors do not improve or students are affected, terminate or nonrenew contracts.

The principals in our studies reported using the following strategies to lessen the influence of a toxic group at faculty meetings:

- Use U-shaped seating with the principal in the center.
- Use a mixer activity to determine seating.
- Put tables together in a circular or oval pattern so we face each other.
- Meet in a circle instead of at tables.
- Make name tents and rearrange them so seating is different at every meeting.
- Divide the teachers into staff development groups and have them sit with their group at meetings; this has been more effective than letting teachers choose their groups.

FOCUSING ON POSITIVE TEACHERS

Return power to positive teachers by focusing on individuals who are hardworking and positive. Make decisions on what is best for the school—not what the negative teachers demand. When school decisions and teacher assignments are made according to the likes and dislikes of difficult teachers, they clearly hold the power in the school. When promising ideas are not pursued because a group of difficult teachers do not like them, difficult behavior is reinforced. Difficult teachers learn that if they complain loudly enough, they will get their way. Ignore their demands and listen to the positive teachers.

Ask everyone to participate—even the difficult teachers. Do not expect the same group of positive, hardworking teachers to shoulder all of the jobs. Avoiding "Martha" because she is disagreeable and giving "Jane" all the tough duties because she is cooperative rewards the difficult teacher and punishes the positive teacher. Likewise, when difficult teachers are not asked to assume the tough jobs and take extra responsibilities, they win again and their negative behaviors are reinforced.

Make Wise Hiring Choices

Hire teachers who are positive. Arrange opportunities for your office assistant, teachers, students, and members of the hiring committee to meet and observe the candidate. During the interview, ask open-ended questions that require candidates to explain their reasoning and decisions.

In addition to the formal interview, arrange opportunities for casual conversations with a variety of staff members. Leave the candidate alone with your office assistant for a few minutes. Invite the candidate to have coffee in a casual setting with a group of teachers. In each instance, have the interviewers or observers listen and watch for signs of negativity. Remember, candidates are on their best behavior. If you detect a hint of negativity during the interview, imagine the negativity that will emerge when they are confronted with the daily demands of teaching.

Protect New Teachers

Negative teachers prey on new teachers. Given the opportunity, a group of difficult teachers can transform an enthusiastic, energetic novice into a cynical, lackluster teacher within a short period of time. Without someone actively providing assistance and a positive direction, struggling new teachers become targets and easy victims.

In addition, experienced teachers who are new to the school and eager to forge new friendships are vulnerable to the influence of difficult teachers who may befriend them. New teachers may struggle to gain acceptance in a school where relationships and friendships are already formed. Team novice and experienced newcomers with positive mentors. Encourage acceptance of new teachers by sharing the contributions the new teachers can make before introducing them to incumbent faculty (Villani, 2008).

The first years of teaching are critical to the long-term development and performance of new teachers. Time invested during the early years of teaching yields huge dividends (Brock & Grady, 2007). The following suggestions may forestall future problems:

- Establish a program that delivers systematic assistance for the first three years of a teacher's career.
- Provide new teachers with mentors who will be positive, supportive, and attentive.
- Position new teachers' classrooms near the office and close to high-performing, enthusiastic veterans.

- Assign new teachers duties and committees that will put them in contact with positive role models.
- Meet regularly with new teachers so they learn your expectations.
- Visit their classrooms and provide feedback.
- Have a frank conversation with them about the dangers and seduction of negativity; emphasize the importance of wise selection of role models and friends.
- Intervene with assistance at the first indication of problems.

Make Teachers a Priority

Maybe I am old fashioned, but simply talking with all faculty frequently and individually goes a long way to creating a healthy work environment.

—An elementary principal

Focus on the people who make student learning possible—the teachers. They are the school's greatest resource; the key to school success. In a job where the demands are many and the visible rewards often few, it is incumbent upon the principal to be the teachers' champion, cheerleader, and coach. Leaders who establish a school culture and climate that meets teachers' needs will be rewarded with loyal, hardworking, and positive teachers. They will have fewer problems with difficult behavior. By contrast, when teachers feel ignored and devalued, the climate becomes optimal for negativity to flourish and toxic subcultures to emerge. Principals, who want to avoid that outcome, make it a priority to focus on teacher satisfaction.

Treat teachers the way you want them to treat students.

Principals do not intentionally forget or ignore teachers' needs. Most principals enter administration with a resolve to remember what it was like to be a teacher and to keep teachers' concerns at the forefront of their decisions. The multiple demands and constraints of the job, however, can easily overshadow that resolve. With paperwork and managerial tasks clamoring for center stage, resolve quickly dwindles; good intentions become distant memories.

Teachers wield the power to make the school a positive learning environment or a denizen of negativity. When teachers are happy and satisfied with their work environment, their performance reflects this satisfaction, and students benefit. Understanding teachers' needs is an important first step.

What Do Teachers Need?

- To feel known and valued as a person
- To be part of a worthwhile endeavor
- To work in a safe and healthy environment
- To be part of a team effort
- To be appreciated for their efforts
- To be recognized for their accomplishments
- To have their ideas and contributions valued
- To be informed about what's going on in the school
- To be included in decisions and changes
- To be offered assistance or coaching when needed

Get to Know Each Teacher

Teachers, like everyone else, want to feel valued. Wise principals get to know each teacher as a person first and a professional second. They make a point of knowing teachers' names, their likes, dislikes, special interests, and something about their families. They greet teachers by name in the hallways, visit their classrooms, ask about their problems, and notice their successes. They seize opportunities for casual conversations; they ask teachers about their families and their personal interests; and, most importantly, they listen to the answers. They welcome teachers when they stop by the office to share a problem, concern, or ask a question. They offer understanding and support when a teacher is ill or dealing with a problem at home. Through these personal contacts, principals establish trusting relationships and communicate to teachers that they are valued. One principal remarked, "It takes time to develop a personal relationship with each teacher, but it is time well spent. I think of it as an investment in the most important resource in my school—the teachers." By contrast, the following teacher remarks illustrate how teachers feel when principals ignore them.

> During my whole first year, my principal never spoke to me or said hello when I passed her in the hallway. I worried for months that she was displeased with my teaching or didn't like me. When I finally shared my concern with a colleague, she said not to worry because the principal didn't talk to anybody; she was usually in a bad mood. I couldn't work in an atmosphere like that. I felt like I was unimportant—not valued as a person. I changed schools.

Principals in our studies reported using the following simple strategies to get to know and develop personal relationships with teachers:

- Going out of one's way to greet individuals on a daily basis
- Asking about personal interests
- Finding out names of spouse, kids, and asking about family
- Celebrating important events in teachers' lives

Principals should remember that teachers have lives outside of school. One teacher said, "My principal keeps telling me I am not a team player because I seldom volunteer for afterschool activities. I would like to, but I have to pick up my small children from day care. Right now, I am doing all I can." Respecting teachers' personal time and encouraging them to take care of their health tells teachers that they are valued as people. Additionally, it ensures that teachers are happier, healthier, and more productive. The following suggestions let teachers know that the principal values them:

- Encouraging teachers to stay home when they are ill.
- Demonstrating understanding when a teacher requests a personal day for a sick child or family member.
- Not holding "surprise" meetings before or after school that disrupt family schedules.
- Dispelling the notion that "good" teachers are expected to be present from sunrise to sunset.

- Keeping afterschool meetings to a stated length.
- Encouraging teachers to carve out time from busy schedules to take care of themselves.
- Rotating extra duties and distributing them fairly among teachers.
- Limiting the number of extra duties that new teachers are assigned.
- Inquiring about circumstances before passing judgment on a teacher's actions.
- Starting an after school exercise class or walking group for teachers.
- Encouraging teachers to read for pleasure by initiating a book club.

Remind Teachers of the Worth of Their Contributions

Teachers need to feel that they are contributing to a worthwhile endeavor, or as Glickman et al. (2005) call it, "a cause greater than oneself" (p. 37). According to Kouzes & Posner (2002), "There is a deep human yearning to make a difference. We want to know that we've done something on this earth, that there's a purpose to our existence" (p. 162). Teachers teach, often in spite of dismally small salaries, because they believe they can make a difference. Teaching gives them purpose and identity; their legacy lives on in their students.

Successful principals repeatedly remind teachers of the worth of the teaching endeavor and the importance of their work. The daily grind of teaching, student discipline problems, and public criticism have a way of obscuring the worth of the larger endeavor.

Make the School Environment Safe and Healthful

If you put good people in bad systems, you get bad results. You have to water the flowers you want to grow.

—Stephen R. Covey

In the most prosperous country in the world, it seems unimaginable that teachers should be expected to teach in schools that compromise their health and safety. Unfortunately, schools exist where teachers are expected to teach in buildings that are environmentally unhealthy and personal safety is a concern. No amount of teacher dedication can or should be expected to overcome such a situation. Teacher turnover in such schools is usually high with teachers migrating to more promising schools. Teachers who remain are at risk of burnout or developing a sense of helplessness that leads to negativity and cynicism. Principals of schools with serious problems need to advocate for immediate improvements in facilities and resources.

Not all schools can be new, modern, and filled with the latest technology. Schools can and do succeed when the principal and teachers are wealthy in spirit, believe they can make a difference, and transmit that belief to students. The difference lies in the talent and commitment of the teachers and the spirit that thrives within the larger school community.

That spirit and dedication rely, in part, on efforts to keep the school safe, clean, adequately maintained, and supplied with appropriate resources. The following suggestions can instill school pride, even in the most impoverished situations:

- Keep the building clean, well maintained, and attractive.
- Maintain adequate security for the building and grounds.
- Be consistent in enforcing a school discipline code.
- Encourage teachers to keep classrooms free of clutter and aesthetically pleasing.
- Engage students in keeping the building clean.
- Introduce the custodial staff to the students; let them know that real people work to keep their building clean.
- At the end of each class, ask students to pick up paper on the floor and straighten desks before leaving.
- Keep the hallways and common areas free of litter.
- Immediately, remove any graffiti, marks, or writing on walls and furniture.
- Advocate for resources, materials, and improvements and make sure teachers and parents are aware of your efforts.

CREATING A SPIRIT OF TEAMWORK

Teamwork is the ability to work together toward a common vision—the ability to direct individual accomplishments toward organizational objectives. It is the fuel that allows common people to attain uncommon results.

—Andrew Carnegie

Everyone wants to play for the winning team. Most teachers look forward to becoming part of a school team and are eager to contribute their talents to a mutual endeavor. They understand that teamwork involves people with a variety of skills and talents working in concert to achieve shared goals. Their mutual respect for each other's talents and their ability to engage in shared learning, mutual planning, goal setting, and socialization provide the synergy that makes success possible.

Difficult teachers, however, often operate outside or on the fringes of the team. Some of them stand at the sidelines, waiting for the team to fail, anxious to say, "I told you that wouldn't work!" Attempts to bring them on board can be challenging but are worth the effort. When difficult teachers begin to feel part of a team, they may be encouraged to suppress individual preferences and needs in favor of those of the group. Much like an athlete in a championship game, the spirit of the team may propel them to abandon selfish concerns for the sake of school success.

The principal plays a key role in generating community spirit and a belief that success is attainable. The principal needs to be the cheerleader for the team. Begin by creating a shared vision and keep everyone working toward the same goal. The following suggestions may be useful:

- Keep everyone focused on the goal. Develop or review the school mission with teachers. Keep the mission short enough so that everyone can remember it; post it in visible places; include it on school documents; refer to it often.
- Maintain an upbeat positive attitude that sustains the group effort. Principals are the cheerleader for the school; smile, keep a positive tone in your voice, have a "can do" attitude, and use a solution-oriented approach to problems.

- Hire front office personnel who are pleasant and helpful and believe that they play a vital role in the endeavor.
- Set high expectations for student learning; convey those expectations to teachers and students.
- Celebrate student learning; recognize and applaud accomplishments. Examine the visible signs of student recognition in your school (e.g., trophies, plaques, award assemblies, school announcements). Do they coincide with the values purported in the school's mission? Are academics rewarded as much as sports?
- Celebrate teacher contributions and achievements.

The principals in our studies felt that developing collegiality and team spirit among faculty were important factors in preventing negative and disruptive teacher behavior. They shared the following suggestions they used to create team spirit:

- Have a family night hosted by staff.
- Develop a program to build trust and collegiality. Teachers nominate each other for monthly awards.
- Order t-shirts with the school name on the back; their grade level is their player number. We wore our team t-shirts to district events.
- Ask for input on things to change and things that should stay the same. That helped immensely with "buy in"— especially for principals new to a school.
- Initiate group activities; share readings and books.
- Talk to every staff member every day.
- Have a monthly celebration after school to celebrate successes.
- Assign peer mentors for new teachers.
- Let the staff know that we may be frustrated by some issues and will work together to overcome the problem.
- Support teachers; teachers don't have to agree with the administration, but they must be able to trust the administration.
- Have staff celebrations, contests, and recognitions to build relationships.
- Bring treats.
- Encourage staff to go into other classrooms. I rotate staff meetings throughout the building.

- During the first staff meeting of the year, I have a scavenger hunt. Teachers are grouped and have to work together to solve clues about where items are located. The scavenger hunt items are all teacher related: plan book, handbook, supplies, and fun things.
- Invite teachers to share experiences about conferences or great summer trips. For example, we had a teacher volunteer at an orphanage in Africa, and she presented a slide show upon her return. It brought many teachers to tears, yet brought everybody together.
- Give everyone an inspirational book to read during the summer, and use the book for small-group discussions throughout the year.
- Identify a theme for each year; hold an opening celebration and present teachers with an item related to the annual theme imprinted with the school name and symbol at the opening meeting (e.g., book bags, school mascot pins, or t-shirts).
- Hold brief faculty socials once a month to bring everyone together.
- Enjoy lighter moments together; laugh; have fun.

REWARDING POSITIVE PEOPLE

A pat on the back is only a few vertebrae removed from a kick in the pants but is miles ahead in results.

—Ella Wheeler Wilcox

Everyone needs to feel appreciated. Teachers are the cornerstone of a school system. However, they are on the lowest rung of the school pyramid, often working under challenging circumstances with inadequate resources. They spend their days isolated in classrooms filled with students of varying needs, circumstances, behaviors, and willingness to learn. After school they prepare lessons, correct papers, meet with parents, attend school meetings, coordinate afterschool activities, and complete paperwork. Some evenings they are back at school attending school functions. The hours are long; the work is challenging; the salary is low; the students are sometimes unwilling; and the public is critical. Calls from disgruntled parents usually out-number notes of appreciation. Although a hug from a kinder-gartener is heartwarming, and a smile from a disgruntled teen is cause for celebration—teachers need, but seldom receive, signs of appreciation from adults. In a study by Beaudoin & Taylor (2004), all of the teachers reported sacrificing personal time to get the job done and feeling resentment about giving much and receiving little appreciation in return. It is no surprise that teachers leave the profession, suffer burnout, and become nega-tive as a result. All people need to feel that their efforts are worthwhile and appreciated.

Maslow told us 50 years ago that needs drive motivation. Yet typically, we assume that people who are doing a good job some-how know that. One retired principal observed, "If I could change one thing that I did as a principal, it would be to thank teachers more for their efforts."

An important part of a leader's responsibility is to show appreciation for teachers' contributions. Appreciation for a job well done is a powerful motivator. According to Kouzes and Posner (2002), "Encouragement . . . is how leaders visibly and behav-iorally link rewards with performance" (p. 18). However, appreci-ation needs to occur year round—not only during Teacher Appreciation Week. Making a teacher feel appreciated does not require excessive time or money. Small gestures can make a differ-ence; making a positive comment, saying thank you, and putting a note in a teacher's mailbox can be the spark that rekindles a teacher's spirit. The important thing is that the remark is genuine and refers to a specific action.

Principals often think they show more appreciation than they actually do, saying that everyday they express appreciation or thank teachers for doing something. However, if there are thirty teachers in the school, in the course of one week, only five of the thirty teachers may receive a gesture of appreciation. Using that same rate of one per day, at the end of the month, five teachers have not heard any words of appreciation. Principals must make a plan to ensure that all teachers' efforts are acknowledged on a consistent basis.

Small gestures for the entire group can go a long way to building morale and creating team spirit. Recruiting volunteers to help with nonteaching tasks gives teachers more time to teach and lets them know that they are appreciated. Celebrating teachers' birthdays with treats, sponsoring monthly socials after school, having pizza delivered for lunch during conferences, delivering "care packages" to beginning teachers, and celebrating career milestones are simple ways to let teachers know that their work is appreciated.

Principals reported the following gestures of appreciation:

- Send positive emails when expectations are met. "Thanks for helping with supervision."
- Thank teachers for helping. "Thanks to those of you who were out in the hall during passing period. I know this takes time you could be using in your room."
- Have a secret committee that has funding for surprises for the staff five to six times per year. Each little gift has a positive saying accompanying it. All staff receive surprises, yet no one knows who delivers them. It's fun and helpful.

Check Your Appreciation Score

We often think we are showing more appreciation than we actually do. If you have 30 or more teachers on your faculty, the teacher-appreciation ratio may be smaller than you think. How many times did you extend a word or gesture of appreciation to an individual teacher during the week? How many times a week do you express appreciation? Check your efforts by keeping a tally for a week. Based on the results, determine a reasonable goal for yourself for the next week.

Appreciation Assessment

Using the following form, record the teacher's name, the work or effort you noted, and the method used (e.g., note, verbal comment). (See also page 149 in the Resources section.)

Appreciation Assessment

	Teachers' Names	*Work or Effort Noted*	*Method of Appreciation*
Mon.	1. 2. 3. 4. 5. 6. 7.		
Tues.	1. 2. 3. 4. 5. 6. 7.		
Wed.	1. 2. 3. 4. 5. 6. 7.		
Thurs.	1. 2. 3. 4. 5. 6. 7.		
Fri.	1. 2. 3. 4. 5. 6. 7.		

As you consider the results of this assessment, what is the difference between the amount of appreciation you thought you expressed and the actual number of times you expressed appreciation during the week?

What strategies can you use to increase the appreciation you express to teachers?

Recognize Teachers for Their Accomplishments

Nothing else can quite substitute for a few well-chosen, well-timed, sincere words of praise. They're absolutely free and worth a fortune.

—Sam Walton

If you want to send the message that you value exemplary performance, praise, recognize, and reward those whose performance warrants it. Celebrate success. Giving recognition for success in addition to showing appreciation for effort, are two strategies that give power to positive teachers.

Teachers are willing to work harder, are more innovative and more productive, and achieve greater satisfaction when they feel successful in their endeavors. Teachers, like everyone else, do what is rewarded and what gives them satisfaction. Whatever is rewarded determines the norm for productivity.

Celebrate your values. If the principal notices and rewards innovative teaching, successful collaboration, and demonstrations of student learning, those behaviors are encouraged and more likely to be repeated. By contrast, ignoring and failing to recognize teacher achievements promotes mediocrity and creates disillusionment, negativity, cynicism, and difficult behaviors. Failure to receive recognition is a leading cause of teacher burnout (Brock & Grady, 2000).

According to Marzano, Water, and McNulty (2005), the egalitarian culture of K–12 education has made the singling out of individuals for recognition somewhat rare. This phenomenon was supported in our studies; few respondents identified recognition as a means of preventing difficult teacher behavior.

Make recognition mean something. Reserve recognition for times when it is earned. Lavishing recognition and praise indiscriminately renders it empty and meaningless. Note a specific accomplishment when offering praise. The words, "You are doing a good job" are nice but meaningless. Be specific in telling teachers what actions are praiseworthy so they can repeat them. Do not limit praise to the two or three superstars on the faculty. Watch for the small accomplishments of teachers who are seldom acknowledged and recognize them.

Decide the appropriateness of making recognition private or public. The context of the situation, the cohesiveness of the faculty, and the personality of the teacher are determinates of the methods you select. Recognizing a teacher's success with an individual student is best kept private; however, success of a more public nature might be shared and celebrated. Be aware that singling out the same teachers repeatedly will contribute to division, competition, jealousy, and an increase in difficult behaviors. If recognitions are public, try to include as many teachers as possible during the course of the year. Suggestions for recognizing teacher achievements include the following:

- Share success stories at faculty meetings.
- Recognize teachers' accomplishments in newsletters.
- Ask teachers to share innovations and strategies with the faculty.
- Encourage teachers to submit articles about successful lessons and innovations to teacher journals.
- Encourage teachers to make presentations at conferences.
- Brag about teachers' accomplishments in presentations to parents.
- Tell teachers' family members about their exemplary performance; invite them to public recognitions.
- Compliment teachers privately.
- Leave complimentary notes in mailboxes.
- Pass on compliments from parents.

Although few participants in our studies included ideas for individual recognition, those who did suggested the following:

- Have a "catch" of the week award to recognize exemplary performance.
- Feature a "Star of the Week" teacher in the weekly newsletter, recognizing a teacher who goes above and beyond normal duties to make class special.

Let Teachers Know Their Talents, Gifts, and Ideas Are Valued

The greatest compliment that was ever paid me was when one asked me what I thought, and attended to my answer.

—Henry David Thoreau

Teachers need to feel that that their contributions make a difference in the school. Wise principals identify and nurture the gifts and talents of each teacher. Sometimes a teacher's difficult behavior may obscure their talents, requiring greater effort on the part of the principal to identify them.

Sometimes difficult behavior is the result of a teacher's talents being thwarted. Talented teachers resent having their ideas ignored and their suggestions discounted. Topchik (2001) refers to them as "caged eagles" and suggests, "When you are lucky enough to find an excellent and motivated performer . . . do not cage them in. Give them the freedom to work on their own and to make important decisions" (pp. 20–21).

Talented teachers whose leadership abilities are stifled may display difficult behaviors usually in the form of complaining about the status quo. Although some teachers complain simply to be complaining, caged eagles complain because they want solutions. Often they have ideas for improvements and will welcome the opportunity to be part of the solution. Unless their abilities are channeled, they will display problem behaviors. Although some of them resort to sabotage, sniping, and anarchy, most of them simply transfer to schools where their leadership can be used. Others seek degrees in school leadership and become principals themselves. Unfortunately, a few of them eventually lose their spirit and becomes victims of burnout (Brock & Grady, 2000).

Consider the Story of Mary Jane

Mary Jane was in her fourth year as a sixth-grade teacher in a large elementary school. She was highly intelligent and well organized and displayed leadership ability. She was a frequent visitor in the principal's office, sharing her concerns that were accompanied with suggestions for improvements. Mr. Jensen, the principal, considered her a major annoyance and treated her with patronizing patience. As soon as she left, he sighed with relief and ignored everything she said. Eventually, Mary Jane became frustrated and outraged; polite suggestions changed to angry demands and outbursts during faculty meetings. Disillusioned, Mary Jane left the school. She took a position in a different school district where the principal identified her as a leader, put her in charge of several initiatives, and encouraged her to pursue graduate studies in educational administration. Today, Mary Jane is using her talents in an administrative position in the central office of a large school district and is pursuing a doctorate.

Principals in our studies reported identifying teacher leaders and placing them in roles of responsibility. The following are strategies they used to develop the talents of their teachers:

- Formed departments and selected chairs to give more ownership to teachers.
- Identified teacher leaders and placed them in appropriate roles of responsibility.
- Identified the strengths of individuals and asked them to take the lead in a project in their area of expertise.
- Asked a teacher to chair a classroom management team for school discipline.
- Had teachers volunteer to lead monthly planning meetings.
- Sent teachers to staff development workshops and asked them to present the information to the rest of the staff.
- Established a principal's advisory council composed of teacher leaders.
- Asked teachers to chair committees, report back to the total staff, and follow through with implementation of plans.
- Enrolled teachers in leadership seminars that led to involving different aspects of school life.
- Assigned a teacher to be coordinator of testing.
- Acknowledged a unit developed by a teacher and asked her to present it at a meeting.
- Assigned leaders for each middle school team.
- Assigned department chairs to lead professional learning community meetings.
- Established book clubs on educational topics with a teacher designated as leader.
- Assigned a teacher leader to be in charge of the school in the principal's absence.

Identification of Teacher Leaders

Consider the teachers in the school and respond to each of the following questions.

- Who are the caged eagles in the building?

- What kinds of leadership activities could be delegated to these eagles?

- How many teachers are serving in leadership positions?

- What activities are teachers leading?

- How could the number of teacher leaders be increased?

- What additional activities could be delegated?

Communicate With Teachers

The problem with communication . . . is the illusion that it has been accomplished.

—George Bernard Shaw

A well-established communication process is a school necessity. Individuals working toward a common goal need to communicate (Fullan, 2001; Leithwood & Riehl, 2003; Marzano et al., 2005). Leaders need to make sure that everyone knows the facts. Technology makes communication easier.

A frequent teacher complaint is the lack of communication between the faculty and the principal. When teachers wonder what is happening or going to happen, rumors begin to fly. Unfortunately, technology also makes it easier to spread rumors.

Teachers attribute communication problems to the following situations:

- Principals do not share problems with teachers, tell them what decisions they are considering, or share decisions that have been made.
- Communication is one-way only—from the principal to the teachers. The opinions and ideas of teachers are not solicited, or teachers' opinions are solicited and then ignored
- The principal's "doom and gloom" attitude and communication style are discouraging and disheartening.

When asked how to prevent difficult behaviors, one principal simply responded, "Communication, communication, and more communication." Wise principals heed this advice and establish a process of regular two-way communication with teachers. They share information, listen, and include teachers' input in their decisions. Before decisions are announced to the larger public, they share them with teachers, offering explanations of how teacher input was factored into the decision. They keep the chain of communication open, involve everyone in discussion, and share information. They feed "facts" to those who manage the "grapevine." They use technology to spread the facts.

Successful principals use a positive and animated style of communication (Kouzes & Posner, 2002). Leaders who communicate information with a positive attitude communicate a "together we can do this" message.

Strategies to facilitate communication include the following:

- Send daily or weekly electronic newsletters using pdf files so information cannot be changed and redistributed. Electronic files of past newsletters enable teachers to review the information they may have missed or want to recheck.
- One principal said, "When I announce a decision or a directive, I always provide a rationale for it."
- Use a whiteboard listing daily events and an inspirational quote.
- Send brief memos to relay important developments or news.
- Have faculty meetings that involve two-way discussions and group decision making.
- Maintain routine personal communication between principal and individual teachers.
- Meet with individual or small groups of teachers prior to the beginning of each schoolyear to gather input and share concerns.
- Share your personal philosophy of leadership and education with teachers so they understand your perspectives and expectations.
- Acknowledge teacher frustrations and assure them that you will all work together toward a resolution.
- Make yourself available for teachers to stop by your office.

Your Communication Strategies

Consider your communication practices and respond to each of the following questions.

- What strategies do you use to share information with teachers?

- What strategies do you use to communicate decisions to teachers?

- What strategies do you use to initiate or welcome personal interactions with teachers?

Provide a Mechanism for Feedback

The participants' perspectives are clouded, while the bystander's views are clear.

—Chinese proverb

As mentioned in the section on communication, teachers want opportunities to provide suggestions, share concerns, and to report problems to the principal. When opportunities and avenues for feedback are not provided, feelings of frustration lead to negativity. Teachers complain to each other whenever and wherever they congregate. Sometimes the complaints reach the ears of parents and other school constituents.

Principals in our studies recognized this need and provided mechanisms for faculty members to offer suggestions and report problems. These approaches included the following:

- Invite faculty to e-mail any concerns; remind them that their voice counts.
- Meet with each teacher at the beginning of the year and two or three times during the year to give them a chance to offer suggestions.
- Form an intervention committee to address conflict.
- Meet monthly with the staff advisory committee and steering committee.
- Meet monthly with the curriculum committee.
- Meet with grade-level teachers three to four times a year.
- Invite team leaders to bring concerns to you.
- Publicize an "open door" policy and be available to hear concerns of individuals or groups.
- Use short surveys via surveymonkey.com to obtain anonymous feedback.

Involve Teachers in Change

None of us is as smart as all of us.

—Japanese proverb

Change is inevitable in school and life. It is not a matter of if we change, but when and how. Regardless of the inevitability or the necessity, change is uncomfortable. For teachers who have spent years using the same curriculum or teaching strategies, change can be upsetting and stressful.

Stress tends to bring out one's worst behavior. Under pressure people resort to earlier behaviors that worked or at least made them feel better—anger, resistance, and avoidance. If teachers do not want a change, they can render it ineffective by refusing to cooperate. Gaining the cooperation of teachers at the beginning of the process is essential.

Involving teachers in the change process gives them a voice in the decision and ownership of the change. The ideas and suggestions teachers offer are essential to decision making in a school. As change is introduced, use the following strategies:

- Explain the reason(s) for the proposed change.
- Share a timeline for the change.
- Cite the benefits of the change to the students.
- Document the research that supports the change.
- Share examples of where the change has worked.
- Provide opportunities for training prior to implementation of the change.
- Involve teachers in planning for the change.

For best results, involve teachers in each aspect of the change process: gathering data about the change; weighing the pros and cons of the change; writing the plan; implementing the plan; and evaluating the results. If the change requires new skills or practices, begin a training program well in advance of the change. The more involvement teachers have in the change and the better prepared they are to make the change, the greater the likelihood that the change will be successful and sustained.

Offer Assistance and Encouragement When Needed

A word of encouragement during a failure is worth more than an hour of praise after success.

—Anonymous

There are times in people's careers when they need assistance and encouragement. We think of new teachers and teachers on improvement plans as needing assistance. However, veteran teachers may require assistance when dealing with curriculum changes or learning a new teaching strategy. Major changes in curriculum, instructional strategies, materials, or technology require training for all teachers in the school. Providing training well in advance of the change will defuse resistance, negativity, and complaining and enable teachers to perform more effectively. One principal said, "We didn't train when we put in a new building communications system—had a ton of complaints. Training was an afterthought, but since then we have not had complaints."

Offering assistance for novice teachers is critical. Becoming a proficient teacher requires practice and can be facilitated by the assistance of a good coach. Novice teachers who are learning new skills want and deserve a helping hand. When new teachers become frustrated and lose their self-confidence, they become disenchanted, disillusioned, and often consider themselves failures. Without assistance, they are likely to become disenchanted and leave teaching. If they remain in the profession, they may align themselves with negative teachers and become the lackluster, difficult teachers of the future.

Remember also that nothing is done perfectly the first time we attempt it. When mistakes or failure occurs, encourage teachers to view them as learning opportunities. Offer assistance and encouragement to try again. The first Dr. Seuss book, now a staple in children's libraries, was rejected by 23 publishers. Fortunately, author Theodor S. Geisel persevered, and the 24th attempt was successful. The book was published and sold six million copies (Kouzes & Posner, 2002). What a loss for the world if he had not persevered. Similarly, what a loss it is for the education profession when fear of failure or lack of assistance inhibits teachers from embracing innovation.

Teachers are often reluctant to ask for assistance. Principals should ask them how they are doing, listen to the answer, and offer help. One principal said, "Every now and then, I visit rooms at the end of the day and just ask teachers how things are going. It opens up lines of communication." Door-opening questions include the following:

- How is your class going?
- What challenges are you experiencing with the new technology?

- How are you doing with the new discipline plan/math curriculum?
- What kind of resources do you need?
- What can I do to help you?

If teachers are unaccustomed to the principal offering assistance, they may initially be reluctant to share their concerns with you. If you offer assistance, be sure to follow through.

Principals shared the following examples of training opportunities they provided for teachers:

- Training prior to initiating new software for online assessments.
- Curriculum mapping trainers were brought in to explain and train the entire staff in how to map courses.
- Workshops on learning communities before initiating them.
- Staff development on a new math program.
- Training on new software and hardware.
- Opportunity for parents to learn new administrative software program before the program "goes live."
- Training on new student information system prior to requiring staff to use it.
- Teachers were asked to pilot a series and become familiar with new curriculum adoptions a year before adoption; they then became trainers for the rest of the faculty.

TAKE ACTION!

- Use the Teacher Assistance form to review your work with teachers.
- Develop a plan to enhance your teacher assistance behavior.
- Identify the indicators of dynamic teamwork in the school.
- Develop a plan to improve the areas where teamwork should be enhanced.

Teacher Assistance

Consider the following questions concerning teacher assistance. Respond to the questions in the space provided.

- What kind of assistance do you provide for beginning teachers?

- What kind of assistance do you provide for teachers on improvement plans?

- Are teachers in your school encouraged to be innovative?

- What was the last innovative idea a teacher tried in your school?

- Is it safe to "fail" in your school?

- Think of the last time a teacher struggled or failed with something. How did you respond?

- How do you find out if teachers are struggling or need assistance?

- What kinds of assistance have you provided recently?

PARTING THOUGHTS: FROM DIFFICULT TEACHERS TO DYNAMIC TEAMWORK

The strategies outlined in this book are not intended as a "quick fix" for teachers' behavior patterns. No amount of effort will eliminate all difficult behavior from the schools. Difficult people have been around for a long time. They have spent years practicing their skills. They are here to stay. Biblical and historical stories recount the conflict and discord they have caused throughout the centuries. However, we should not condone this behavior in the schools.

Influencing a teacher to change a negative behavior takes time, perseverance, repeated attempts, and a variety of strategies. Sometimes you will not succeed in spite of your best attempts! However, it is worth the effort. We hope that you will *confront* teachers who are difficult, *reinforce* teachers who are positive, and *build* dynamic teamwork in the schools. The success of our schools is far too important not to give it our best effort.

Resources

Behavior Change Plan

The objectionable behavior: _____

The reward for the behavior: _____

The targeted new behavior: _____

Past strategies: _____

The new strategy: _____

PART 1: TEACHER'S EVALUATION
OF THE PRINCIPAL'S PERFORMANCE

Check the appropriate column using the following scale:

5 = Outstanding; 4 = Exceeds expectations; 3 = Satisfactory; 2 = Needs improvement; 1 = Unsatisfactory

Teacher's Evaluation of the Principal's Performance					
THE PRINCIPAL:	5	4	3	2	1
Values me as a person					
Respects me as a teacher					
Listens to my needs and problems					
Appreciates my efforts					
Treats me fairly					
Avoids favoritism					
Recognizes my achievements					
Encourages my professional growth					
Listens objectively to input from teachers					
Shares decision making					
Follows through on decisions					
Keeps promises					
Is trustworthy					
Demonstrates emotional stability					
Keeps personal problems out of school					
Distributes duties fairly					
Is visible in the building					

PART 2: TEACHER'S EVALUATION OF THE PRINCIPAL'S PERFORMANCE

Average the scores of the teachers' evaluations of the principal. Circle the average score for each item from Part 1. For items with an average of 2 (needs improvement) or 1 (unsatisfactory), determine the changes you want to make to improve your performance in that area.

Teacher's Evaluation of the Principal's Performance		
THE PRINCIPAL:	*Score*	*Changes I will make to improve performance:*
Values me as a person	5 4 3 2 1	
Respects me as a teacher	5 4 3 2 1	
Listens to my needs and problems	5 4 3 2 1	
Appreciates my efforts	5 4 3 2 1	
Treats me fairly	5 4 3 2 1	
Avoids favoritism	5 4 3 2 1	
Recognizes my achievements	5 4 3 2 1	
Encourages my professional growth	5 4 3 2 1	
Listens objectively to input from teachers	5 4 3 2 1	
Shares decision making	5 4 3 2 1	
Follows through on decisions	5 4 3 2 1	
Keeps promises	5 4 3 2 1	
Is trustworthy	5 4 3 2 1	
Demonstrates emotional stability	5 4 3 2 1	
Keeps personal problems out of school	5 4 3 2 1	
Distributes duties fairly	5 4 3 2 1	
Is visible in the building	5 4 3 2 1	

EVALUATION OF LISTENING SKILLS

Use the following rating sheet to conduct a self-evaluation; then ask teachers to evaluate you.

Check the appropriate rating for each statement:

5 = Outstanding; 4 = Exceeds expectations; 3 = Satisfactory; 2 = Needs improvement; 1 = Unsatisfactory

Teacher's Evaluation of the Principal: Listening Skills					
THE PRINCIPAL:	*5*	*4*	*3*	*2*	*1*
Is a good listener.					
Seems pleased when I ask to speak with him or her.					
Stops working; gives me full attention when I am speaking.					
Is interested in what I am saying.					
Listens without interrupting me.					
Asks questions to clarify my message.					
Repeats my message to check for understanding.					

EVALUATION OF SPEAKING SKILLS

Use the following rating sheet to conduct a self-evaluation; then ask teachers to evaluate you.

Check the appropriate rating for each statement:

5 = Outstanding; 4 = Exceeds expectations; 3 = Satisfactory; 2 = Needs improvement; 1 = Unsatisfactory

Teacher's Evaluation of the Principal: Speaking Skills					
THE PRINCIPAL:	5	4	3	2	1
Is an engaging and interesting speaker.					
Responds to questions with clear and concise answers.					
Gets to the point when sharing information.					
Uses language that is easily understood.					
Answers questions or e-mails in a respectful tone of voice.					
Checks for understanding and offers necessary clarification.					

Appreciation Assessment

Record the teacher's name, the work or effort you noted, and the method used (e.g., note, verbal comment).

	Teachers' Names	Work or Effort Noted	Method of Appreciation
Mon.	1. 2. 3. 4. 5. 6. 7.		
Tues.	1. 2. 3. 4. 5. 6. 7.		
Wed.	1. 2. 3. 4. 5. 6. 7.		
Thurs.	1. 2. 3. 4. 5. 6. 7.		
Fri.	1. 2. 3. 4. 5. 6. 7.		

Identification of Teacher Leaders

Consider the teachers in the school and respond to each of the following questions.

- Who are the caged eagles in the building?

- What kinds of leadership activities could be delegated to these eagles?

- How many teachers are serving in leadership positions?

- What activities are teachers leading?

- How could the number of teacher leaders be increased?

- What additional activities could be delegated?

Your Communication Strategies

Consider your communication practices and respond to each of the following questions.

- What strategies do you use to share information with teachers?

- What strategies do you use to communicate decisions to teachers?

- What strategies do you use to initiate or welcome personal interactions with teachers?

Teacher Assistance

Consider the following questions concerning teacher assistance. Respond to the questions in the space provided.

- What kind of assistance do you provide for beginning teachers?

- What kind of assistance do you provide for teachers on improvement plans?

- Are teachers in your school encouraged to be innovative?

- What was the last innovative idea a teacher tried in your school?

- Is it safe to "fail" in your school?

- Think of the last time a teacher struggled or failed with something. How did you respond?

- How do you find out if teachers are struggling or need assistance?

- What kinds of assistance have you provided recently?

References

Aldrich, N. (2002). *Taming the difficult employee.* Retrieved July 15, 2008, from http://www.lib.niu.edu/2002/ip020522.html.

Andersen, H. A. (1837). Keiserens nye kloeder (The emperor has no clothes). In *Eventyr, fortalte for Børn* (Fairytales told for children), (Jean Hersholt, Trans.). Retrieved April 16, 2008, from http://www.andersen.sdu.dk/vaerk/hersholt/TheEmperorsNewClothes_e.html.

Anderson, B. (1995, Dec.). Less gossip, better schools. *Education Digest, 61*(4), 9–22.

Bassman, E. S. (1992). *Abuse in the workplace: Management remedies and bottom line impact.* New York: Quorum.

Beaudoin, M. N., & Taylor, M. (2004). *Creating a positive school culture.* Thousand Oaks, CA: Corwin.

Bell, A. H., & Smith, D. M. (2002). *Winning with difficult people* (3rd ed.). Hauppage, NY: Barron's Educational Series.

Bell, A. H., & Smith, D. M. (2004). *Winning with difficult people.* Hauppauge, NY: Barron's Educational Series.

Blase, J., & Blase, J. (2003). *Breaking the silence: Overcoming the problem of principal mistreatment of teachers.* Thousand Oaks, CA: Corwin.

Bolton, R. (1979). *People skills.* NY: Simon & Schuster.

Bramson, R. M. (1981). *Coping with difficult people.* Garden City, NY: Anchor Press/Doubleday.

Brinkman, R., & Kirschner, R. (2002). *Dealing with people you can't stand.* New York: McGraw Hill.

Brock, B. L. (2008, April). When sisterly collaboration turns to sabotage. Paper presented to the Nebraska Women in Higher Education Leadership State Conference, Bellevue, NE.

Brock, B. L. (2008, July). When sisterly support changes to sabotage. *Journal of Women in Educational Leadership, 6*(3), 211–226.

Brock, B. L., & Grady, M. L. (1995). *Principals in transition: Tips for surviving succession.* Thousand Oaks, CA: Corwin.

Brock, B. L., & Grady, M. L. (2000). *Rekindling the flame: Principals combating teacher burnout.* Thousand Oaks, CA: Corwin.

Brock, B. L., & Grady, M. L. (2002). *Avoiding burnout.* Thousand Oaks, CA; Corwin.

Brock, B. L., & Grady, M. L. (2006). Dealing with negative and disruptive teachers: Strategies for administrators. *International Journal of Education (online), 12*(3), 323–334. Retrieved Dec. 15, 2008, from http://ijl.cgpublisher.com/product/pub.30/prod.590

Brock, B. L., & Grady, M. L. (2007). *From first-year to first-rate: Principals guiding beginning teachers* (3rd ed.). Thousand Oaks, CA: Corwin.

Canter, L., & Canter, M. (1976). *Assertive discipline: A take-charge approach for today's educator.* Los Angeles, CA: Canter and Associates.

Chesler, P. (2001). *Women's inhumanity to women.* New York: Thunder's Mouth Press.

Condrill, J., & Bough, B. B. (2007). *101 ways to improve your communication skills instantly* (4th ed.). San Antonio, TX: GoalMinds.

Culver, M. K. (2007). Relational aggression and burnout: Fight, hide, or run? *Journal of Women in Educational Leadership, 5*(3), 163–182.

Deal, T. E., & Peterson, K. D. (1998). *Shaping school culture: The heart of leadership.* San Francisco, CA: Jossey-Bass.

French, Jr., J. R. P., & Raven, B. (1959). The bases of social power. In *Studies in Social Power* (150–167), edited by Dorwin P. Cartwright. Ann Arbor, MI: Institute for Social Research, The University of Michigan.

Fullan, M. (2001). *Leading in a culture of change.* San Francisco: Jossey-Bass.

Gill, L. (1999). *How to work with just about anyone.* New York: Simon & Schuster.

Gilligan, C. (1982). *In a different voice.* Cambridge, MA: Harvard University Press.

Glickman, C. G., Gordon, S. P., & Ross-Gordon, J. M. (2005). *The basic guide to supervision and instructional leadership.* Boston: Allyn & Bacon.

Glickman, C. G., Gordon, S. P., & Ross-Gordon, J. M. (2007). *Supervision and instructional leadership.* Boston: Pearson.

Glickman, C. G., Gordon, S. P., & Ross-Gordon, J. M. (2009). *Supervision and instructional leadership.* Boston: Pearson.

Gouldner, A. W. (1954). *Patterns of industrial democracy.* Glencoe, IL: Free Press.

Heim, P., Murphy, S. A., & Golant, S. K. (2001). *In the company of women.* New York: Tarcher/Putnam.

Herzberg, F. (1968, January/February). One more time: How do you motivate employees? *Harvard Business Review, 47,* 53–62.

Joyce, B., & Showers, B. (2002). *Student achievement through staff development.* Alexandria, VA: Association for Supervision and Curriculum Development.

Kosmoski, G. J., & Pollack, D. R. (2000). *Managing difficult, frustrating, and hostile conversations.* Thousand Oaks, CA: Corwin.

Kouzes, J. M., & Posner, B. Z. (2002). *Leadership challenge* (3rd ed.) San Francisco, CA: Jossey-Bass.

Lawrence, C. E. (2005). *The marginal teacher: A step-by-step guide to fair procedures for identification and dismissal* (3rd ed.). Thousand Oaks, CA: Corwin.

Lawrence C. E., & Vachon, M. K. (2003). *How to handle staff misconduct* (2nd ed.). Thousand Oaks, CA: Corwin.

Leithwood, K. A., & Riehl, C. (2003). What do we already know about successful school leadership: Review of research. Paper presented at the annual meeting of the American Educational Research Association, Chicago, IL.

Luft, J., & Ingham, H. (1955). The Johari window, a graphic model of interpersonal awareness, *Proceedings of the Western Training Laboratory in Group Development*. Los Angeles, CA: UCLA.

Marzano, R. J., Water, T., & McNulty, B. A. (2005). *School leadership that works: From research to results.* Aurora, CO: Mid-continent Research for Education and Learning.

Negotiation Skills Company. (2003). Dealing with Difficult People. Retrieved April 16, 2008, from http://www.negotiationskills.com.

Oxford Dictionary. (1997). London: Oxford University Press.

Pawlas, G. E., & Oliva, P. F. (2008). *Supervision for today's schools.* New York: John Wiley and Sons.

Peterson, K. D. (1999). Time use flows from school culture: River of values and traditions can nurture or poison staff development hours. *Journal of Staff Development, 20*(2). Retrieved July 17, 2008 from http://www.nsdc.org/library/publications/jsd/peterson202.cfm.

Peterson, K. D., & Deal, T. E. (2002). *Shaping school culture fieldbook.* San Francisco, CA: Jossey-Bass.

Podestra, C., & Sanderson, V. (1999). *Life would be easy if it weren't for other people.* Thousand Oaks, CA: Corwin.

Schermerhorn, J. R., Jr., Hunt, J. G., & Osborn, R. N. (2008). *Organizational behavior.* Jefferson City: R. R. Donnelly.

Scott, S. (2004). *Fierce conversations: Achieving success at work and in life, one conversation at a time.* New York: Berkley.

Sergiovanni, T. J., & Starratt, R. J. (2002). *Supervision: A redefinition* (7th ed.). New York: McGraw-Hill.

Stone, D., Patton, B., & Heen, S. (2000). *Difficult conversations: How to discuss what matters most.* New York: Penguin Books.

Tanenbaum, L. (2002). *Catfight.* New York: Harper Collins.

Ting-Tooney, S. (1979). Gossip as a communication construct. Paper presented at the annual meeting of the Western Speech Communication Association. Los Angeles, CA, February 17, 1979. ED224069.

Topchik, G. S. (2001). *Managing workplace negativity.* New York: AMACOM.

Villani, S. (2008) *Are you sure you are the principal? A guide for new and aspiring leaders* (2nd ed.). Thousand Oaks, CA: Corwin.

Wagner, C. R. (2004, Fall/2005, Winter). Leadership for an improved school culture, *Kentucky School Leader*, 9–16, Retrieved Dec. 15, 2008, from http://www.schoolculture.net/kyschoolleaderfall04.pdf.

Index

Active listening, 98
Administrative behavior.
   See Difficult principals
Administrative solutions:
  administrator attrition, 22–23, 70
  anarchists, 41
  behavioral analysis, 56–57
  behavioral motivation, 53–54
  behavioral prevention strategies,
    51–56
  Behavior Change Plan, 58, 59, 144
  classroom visits, 52
  complainers, 27–29, 30, 61–64
  difficult principals, 85, 86–88
  formal procedures, 64–70
  gossipers, 37, 38, 39–40
  imperative action, 55–56
  inflexibility, 33–34
  intimidators, 44–46, 66–68
  negativity, 31–32, 65–66
  noisemakers, 46–48
  noncompliance, 34–35
  personal attitude, 52–53, 55
  problem avoidance, 18–21, 54
  purposeful conversation, 60–64
  remediation meeting, 59–64
  selfishness, 48
  snipers, 42–43
  Take Action strategies, 70
  teacher attrition, 21–22, 69
  teacher rapport, 51–52, 118–120
  teacher removal, 60, 68–70
  teacher termination, 69–70
  teacher transfer, 68–69
  See also Communication skills;
    Teamwork

Aggressive behavior,
  14, 15, 16–17, 34
Anarchists, 7, 11, 40–41
  administrative solutions, 41
Assertive behavior, 14, 15
Attrition:
  administrators, 22–23, 70
  teachers, 21–22, 69
Authoritarian management,
  72–73, 74

Backbiters, 8, 12, 17, 38–40
Behavioral strategies. *See*
    Administrative solutions;
    Communication skills;
    Teamwork
Behavioral styles:
  aggressive behavior,
    14, 15, 16–17, 34
  assertive behavior, 14, 15
  passive-aggressive behavior,
    14, 15, 16–18, 34, 80
  passive behavior, 15, 16–17
Behavior Change Plan, 58, 59, 144
Body language, 102–103
Bullying, 43–46
  See also Intimidators

Chatterboxes, 36–37
Classroom visits, 52
Communication skills:
  body language, 102–103
  difficult principals, 76, 77
  emotionally charged
    conversations, 103–107
  listening strategies, 93–98

message transmittal, 94–95
nonverbal language, 102–103
purposeful conversation, 60–64
speaking strategies, 99–101
strategy questionnaire, 135, 151
Take Action strategies, 107
teacher rapport, 51–52, 118–120
teamwork, 133–135
trusting relationships, 93–94
violent threats, 106–107
Complainers, 7, 10, 14, 25–30
     administrative solutions, 27–29,
          30, 61–64
     example of, 26–27, 28–29, 61–64
     faculty room complainer, 30
     group complainers, 30
     in-your-face complainer, 26–29
Contagious behavior, 19–21

Delegation skills, 76, 77
Difficult behaviors:
     anarchy, 7, 11, 40–41
     backbiting, 8, 12, 17, 38–40
     bullying, 43–46
     complaining, 7, 10, 14, 25–30,
          60–64
     defined, 8
     gender differences, 14, 17–18
     gossiping, 7, 11, 14, 16, 17, 35–40
     inflexibility, 7, 10, 32–34
     intimidating, 8, 12–13, 14,
          43–46, 66–68
     negativity, 7, 10, 31–32, 65–66
     noisemaking, 8, 11–12, 46–48
     noncompliance, 7, 10–11, 14,
          34–35
     sabotage, 17–18, 80, 84–85
     selfish, 8, 13, 48
     sniping, 8, 12, 16, 17, 42–43
     Take Action strategies, 48
     tyrannical, 8, 12, 44
     See also Administrative solutions
Difficult principals:
     administrative solutions,
          85, 86–88
     authoritarian management,
          72–73, 74

behavioral blind-spot, 72–73
behavioral manifestation, 76–78
causation factors, 73–75
communication skills, 76, 77
defensiveness, 76, 78
delegation skills, 76, 77
emotional stability, 76, 78
favoritism, 76, 78
follow-through, 76, 78
gender differences, 82–85
humor, 86–87
inexperience, 73–74
listening skills, 76, 77, 88
popularity problem, 73, 74
power addiction, 73, 75
rigid management, 76
school climate, 71–72, 78–82
self-monitoring tools, 87–88
shared decision making, 86
supervisory feedback, 88
Take Action strategies, 88
teacher evaluation, 87–88,
     89, 90, 145, 146
teacher feedback,
     86, 87–88, 136
teacher reaction, 75, 87
teacher recognition, 76, 77, 86
teacher relationships, 86
Difficult teachers:
     behavioral development, 13–15
     behavioral effects, 17–23
     behavioral rationale, 15
     behavioral styles, 14, 15–18,
          34, 80
     cautionary advice, 17
     contagious behavior, 19–21
     identification of, 7–13
     Take Action strategies, 23
     toxic subcultures, 19, 30, 75, 80,
          81, 94
     See also Administrative solutions;
          Teamwork

Emotionally charged
     conversations,
          100–101, 103–107
Emotional stability, 76, 78

Faculty room complainer, 30
Favoritism, 76, 78
Follow-through, 76, 78

Gender differences:
  difficult behaviors, 14, 17–18
  difficult principals, 82–85
  gossipers, 35–36
Gossipers, 7, 11, 14, 16, 17, 35–40
  administrative solutions, 37, 38,
    39–40
  backbiters, 38–40
  causation factors, 35–36
  chatterboxes, 36–37
  effects of, 36
  example of, 39–40
  gender differences, 35–36
  goals of, 35, 36
  gossiping origination, 35
  tattletales, 37–38
Group complainers, 30

How to Handle Staff Misconduct
    (Lawrence and Vachon), 64
Humor, 86–87

Inexperienced principals, 73–74
Inflexibility, 7, 10, 32–34
  administrative solutions, 33–34
Interpersonal skills. *See*
    Communication skills; Listening
    skills; Speaking skills
Intimidators, 8, 12–13, 14, 43–46,
    66–68
  administrative solutions, 44–46,
    66–68
  example of, 44–45, 66–68
In-your-face complainer, 26–29

Lawrence, C. E., 64
Listening skills:
  active listening, 98
  communication strategies, 93–98
  comprehension, 97
  difficult principals, 76, 77, 88
  door-openers, 96
  evaluation template, 108, 147

information evaluation, 97
  judgments, 97
  reflection, 97
  silent listening, 96
  speaker welcoming-strategies, 96
  value of, 97–98

Marginal Teacher, The (Lawrence), 64

Negativity, 7, 10, 31–32, 65–66
  administrative solutions,
    31–32, 65–66
  example of, 65–66
Noisemakers, 8, 11–12, 46–48
  administrative solutions, 46–48
Noncompliance, 7, 10–11, 14,
    34–35
  administrative solutions,
    34–35
Nonverbal language, 102–103

Passive-aggressive behavior,
    14, 15, 16–18, 34, 80
Passive behavior, 15, 16–17
Power addiction, 73, 75
Preservice teachers, 14–15
Principals. *See* Administrative
    solutions; Communication
    skills; Difficult principals;
    Teamwork

Remediation meeting, 59–64
Resources:
  Behavior Change Plan,
    58, 59, 144
  communication skills
    questionnaire, 135, 151
  difficult-principal causes, 73–75
  difficult-teacher strategies,
    60–70
  nonverbal cues, 103
  teacher assistance questionnaire,
    140, 152
  teacher leadership questionnaire,
    132, 150
  See also Templates
Rigid management, 76

Sabotage, 17–18, 80, 84–85
School climate:
   difficult principals, 71–72, 78–82
   environmental safety, 120–121
   teamwork, 111–115
Selfishness, 8, 13, 48
   administrative solutions, 48
Shared decision making, 86
Snipers, 8, 12, 16, 17, 42–43
   administrative solutions, 42–43
   example of, 42, 43
Speaking skills:
   communication purpose, 99
   communication strategies, 99–101
   emotionally charged words,
      100–101
   evaluation template, 109, 148
   listener considerations, 99
   message conveyance, 99–100
   precise language, 100–101
   tone of voice, 101
Student learning, 8, 18, 44

Tattletales, 37–38
Teachers:
   administrative rapport, 51–52,
      118–120
   appreciation assessment template,
      127, 149
   appreciation score, 126
   assistance questionnaire, 140, 152
   attrition, 21–22, 69
   contribution value, 130–132
   favoritism, 76, 78
   feedback, 86, 87–88, 136
   leadership appreciation,
      130–132, 150
   leadership questionnaire, 132, 150
   principal evaluation, 87–88, 89,
      90, 145, 146
   recognition, 76, 77, 86, 120,
      124–139
   removal of, 60, 68–70
   termination of, 69–70

   transfer of, 68–69
   See also Difficult behaviors; Difficult
      teachers; Teamwork
Teamwork:
   communication strategies, 133–135
   contribution value, 130–132
   dynamic teamwork, 141
   environmental safety, 120–121
   feedback, 136
   group effort, 114
   hiring choices, 115–116
   new-teacher support, 116–117
   positive school cultures, 111–115
   positive teachers, 115–121,
      124–139
   prioritized teachers, 117–118
   Take Action strategies, 139
   teacher accomplishments,
      128–129
   teacher assistance,
      137–139, 140, 152
   teacher involvement, 136–137
   teacher leadership, 130–132, 150
   teacher needs, 118
   teacher rapport, 118–120
   teacher recognition,
      120, 124–139
   team spirit strategies, 122–124
   toxic subcultures, 113–115
Templates:
   Behavior Change Plan, 58, 144
   listening skills evaluation, 108, 147
   principal evaluation,
      89, 90, 145, 146
   speaking skills evaluation, 109, 148
   teacher appreciation assessment,
      127, 149
   See also Resources
Toxic subcultures,
      19, 30, 75, 80, 81, 94
Tyranny, 8, 12, 44

Vachon, M. K., 64
Violent threats, 106–107

CORWIN

A SAGE Company

The Corwin logo—a raven striding across an open book—represents the union of courage and learning. Corwin is committed to improving education for all learners by publishing books and other professional development resources for those serving the field of PreK–12 education. By providing practical, hands-on materials, Corwin continues to carry out the promise of its motto: **"Helping Educators Do Their Work Better."**

The mission of the National Association of Elementary School Principals is to lead in the advocacy and support for elementary and middle level principals and other education leaders in their commitment for all children.